Crash The Early Warning

Major economic and social changes are coming like a missile from space, forecasting America's future based on economics, weather cycles and long-term stock market trends.

Crash The Early Warning

A quick study of the causes of stock market failures, recessions, booms and the cyclical forces that control economic activity, weather, climate and much mass social behavior.

Robert Earl Andrews
Economist and Market Consultant

Writer's Showcase

San Jose New York Lincoln Shanghai

Crash The Early Warning

Writer's Showcase
an imprint of iUniverse, Inc.

For information address:
iUniverse, Inc.
5220 S. 16th St., Suite 200
Lincoln, NE 68512
www.iuniverse.com

Cover design by APT Graphic Design,
author photo by Hicks Custom Photography.

ISBN: 0-595-21984-5

Printed in the United States of America

"The past dictates the future."
—Andrews

Contents

List of Illustrations xi

Foreword xiii

Preface xix

CHAPTER 1   When Are Taxes Too Much?. 1

CHAPTER 2   Tipping the Scales 16

CHAPTER 3   Free Money is Never Free 20

CHAPTER 4   Importance of Cycles. 21

CHAPTER 5   Can We Trust the Cycles? 39

CHAPTER 6   Coming Energy Crisis 41

CHAPTER 7   Population is in Free Fall. 43

CHAPTER 8   Federal Reserve Board Seems Helpless. 45

CHAPTER 9   Chinese Threat Remains 51

CHAPTER 10   A Debilitating Monopoly: OPEC 53

CHAPTER 11   Inflation! Inflation? 60

CHAPTER 12   Collusion. 62

CHAPTER 13   Inflation Will Now Follow 64

CHAPTER 14   Inflation Under President Johnson 66

CHAPTER 15   The OPEC Monopolies are
             Arab-Dominated 69

CHAPTER 16   Immigration Problems and Coming
Change 72

CHAPTER 17   Immigration Trends 77

CHAPTER 18   Border Controls 79

CHAPTER 19   Threat to U.S. Security is from Within 83

CHAPTER 20   Where the Great Risk Abounds. 86

CHAPTER 21   Anarchist Day of Infamy. 88

CHAPTER 22   Evidence of Big Changes Coming. 92

CHAPTER 23   Climate Myopia: Global Warming? 98

CHAPTER 24   Confirming the Shift to Conservatism 100

CHAPTER 25   Crash of 2008 103

CHAPTER 26   Educational Failures and Changes Needed 105

CHAPTER 27   Election 2000, a Cultural Turn Signal 108

CHAPTER 28   Energy Prices: Cause and Effect 110

CHAPTER 29   Gasoline, Food and Energy Shortfall. 115

CHAPTER 30   Gerrymandering Will End the Liberal. 119

CHAPTER 31   Governor Gray Davis, California 121

CHAPTER 32   Hoof & Mouth Disease, a Threat 122

CHAPTER 33   Hoof & Mouth Disease Discovery 123

CHAPTER 34   Housing, Homes and Construction 125

CHAPTER 35   Leadership Shifts Dominate, Trends
Change 130

CHAPTER 36   Liberal Wing of Democratic Party 131

CHAPTER 37   Line Budgeting—Integrity in
Government 132

CHAPTER 38   Mad Cow Disease and Man 134

CHAPTER 39   Media Excesses, Without Facts 136

CHAPTER 40   Minimum Wage is Inflationary 142

CHAPTER 41   National Energy Policy Versus OPEC 143

CHAPTER 42   New Age is Coming, Now 148

CHAPTER 43   Presidential Candidates 151

CHAPTER 44   Reliable Government Data 154

CHAPTER 45   Educational Misadventures 155

CHAPTER 46   Soft Money 163

CHAPTER 47   Is Weather or Climate Changing? 165

CHAPTER 48   Who's Responsible for Depressions? 166

CHAPTER 49   Long-Term Market Trend Reversal Signals, a
Look at the Future. 173

CHAPTER 50   The Coming Energy Crisis is Here, Now! 184

CHAPTER 51   Water Rights of the West 190

CHAPTER 52   Let's Look at a Bit of Historical Fact 193

CHAPTER 53   Socialism Versus Capitalism 197

CHAPTER 54   How Does Totalitarianism Start? 200

CHAPTER 55   The High Risk Period is Year 2008-10 203

About the Author 205

List of Illustrations

Chart 1—37-Year Stock Market Cycle *24*

Chart 2—Stock Market with 4-year, 18-year and 11-year Weather Cycles *36*

Foreword

All progress comes from sorting out irrelevant elements of society and correcting errors of predecessor laws and customs. To achieve this progress, man, often reluctantly, must dispose of backward antiquated agriculture, religious, social or industry-based customs, beliefs and concepts for a greater opportunity to fulfill an unsuspected destiny. Real change usually is swift and sudden, breaking down all barriers. New products like gunpowder, aircraft, missiles, night vision, satellites, computers, the internet, a new political philosophy, a resurgence of a religious idea often alter the relationships of one nation to others.

Wars frequently occur at such times to destroy the past in a region. We are seeing this in Yugoslavia, Russia, Afghanistan, Palestine and Israel, Syria, Iran and even in Libya. Backward regions and states when mobilized to maximize their potential for their citizens rapidly discard old customs breaking the chains of religious leaders, social philosophy, Nomadic wandering habits to survive and find a greater reason for living. They may soon prosper and engage in creative science ventures and new social relationships of a modern society. The new generation leaves the aging generation to learn about success and then participate in believing their personal ability to prosper.

The laws and social standards of a society, having eroded, must be replaced with better standards of living and revisions to dominate social philosophy else, it degrades all societies. Each of us must find our place in a culture to express our true worth. Whatever a person does to participate in the life experience on this earth is an outer expression of what is inborn, in the genetic code, inbred and disciplined to express and exceed the standards of the past. The local culture then bends the personality to fit the village.

It is not some sort of indoctrination that hampers social change, but the agenda bias of political and religious social control that keeps us tied and chained to false beliefs. We are slaves of the political correctness of the times and of vested interests of the past in which we live. Break the chains that bind you. Become a leader or go to school and specialize in a trade or profession. Think!

Under Islam, the rituals are the chains of control by the clerics. Ancient religions tend to emphasize rituals, holy days and pageantry of the belief. Priests, politicians and clerics write the rules and force the people, the "believers" to tithe and follow their laws. In many religions, those who do not follow are killed, forced out of the church (excommunicated) or excluded from local social affairs, perhaps tribal dances, hunts, jobs, celebrations, rituals, etc.

The Christian religion follows similar practices, but appears to be less brutish today than does Islam. This is our modern frame of reference. Religion was invented to guide the cult, kingdom or clan called our town or society with civil customs and mores relating to each other.

We carry our entire physical baggage from our past in our genes, which constantly stipulate how we shall pursue our lives. Perhaps some of us are survivors of ancient civilizations as found in lineage known only to have existed in archaeological digs to be guides to the future. Latent physical, mental and personal traits seem to erupt in some of our children with characteristics right out of untold years in the past.

We moved from a hunting and gathering society, often clubbing food to death, then learned to use spears, arrows, bullets, lasers, missiles, guided missiles and psychological warfare to overcome opposition to meet our needs and to hold our territory. We devise these new methods from our experiences then put them into our own understanding of how to achieve in the future.

One day we will reach outward into space as easily as we use a radio, cellular phones and television signals to communicate. Soon we will use the energy sources of earth's own magnetic fields to drive our vehicles on earth without using oil and we will do the same flying into the heavens with solar magnetic energy.

We stand on the shoulders of forefathers who fought the oppressors and created free lands and mutual laws to equalize authority moving away from autocratic leadership of kings, bureaucrats, dictators, clerics, popes and despots.

Western science will support improvements in the future but must fight to keep tyranny from again ruling our nations. In a sense, the scientific community has replaced the law of religions with provable concepts of how things actually work. Likewise, the Constitution replaced much of the religious dogma of the clerical religious bureaucracy and organization and lowers the need for the populations to believe in a religion or a god. Even when Pontius Pilot washed his hands of the Jesus affair, he relinquished the right of Roman authority to pass judgment on matters of religion and theocracy. Politically the division of government then split away from controlling personal thought and modern civilization began.

At the beginning of this third millennium, we are engaged in a ferocious emotional and philosophical struggle to validate our modern capitalist system and our freedom of thought, worship and action. It is this battle of religious dogma that has failed its believers for 1300 years, leaving them only with their catechism of indoctrination from Muhammad, and leaving them out of the scientific revolution.

This separation appears to have begun about the time they were ejected from European lands back into Africa. It is a greater battle today than the world fighting the drug debauchery of our past, control by authoritarian threat and religious schemes. The emotional baggage among cultures often helds back any new idea or discovery that could loosen the chains of mental slavery, often limiting our understanding of the heavenly forces we seek and pray for. We seem to need a war for each generation wherein the young become engaged in sharpening their life values, leaving the past behind and developing respect for their nation and its way of life.

We must engage in research to find ways to enhance all mankind to travel to other worlds and into ventures never dreamed of before. Whether we will prevail against an indoctrinated world of hate, religious bigotry, vengeance, divisive leadership, Jihad mentality, and monopolistic oil control, it is in our future to fight for or to lose our freedoms by inaction or political bigotry and stupidity. This is the state of western man today in his struggle for dominance of nature and to remain free.

In the mind of one's worldly friends, associates and libraries with different concepts of the past, we gain delivery of different history in books, archaeology and experiments to help fill our need to order our thoughts into today's jargon of language. History still repeats, only the people change names, jobs and addresses in their migration and trans-migration toward prosperity and growth.

The author wishes to thank professors and doctors of knowledge who, during their learning years saw through much of the confused thinking found in their own experience to pass greater understanding onto our modern generation giving it a sharper edge. In today's age the author's associates, aides and friends were very helpful in guiding the author's expression of these powerful forces into this book.

Thanks to Ed, Don, Gregg, John, Tom, Ryan, Irma, Estelle and Phyllis; reference librarians of untold libraries; Edward R. Dewey author of "Cycles," Joseph A. Schumpeter for his work in "Business Cycles," Immanuel Velikovsky for his historical vision of events, Martin Mayer for his financial works and "The Bankers" and other writers gleaning valuable ideas then presenting them in writing for those who were searching for reason in this make-shift world we live in today.

John Maynard Keynes of England defined much of the economic theory in practice today that is managed by The FRB (Federal Reserve Board) in the United States. Nobel economic laureate Paul Samuelson theorized many new variations, but did not suspect the tremendous guiding power found in the general theory of cycles around which this data is formatted.

Major change often comes suddenly, unannounced and violently. The destruction of the World Trade Center was the fourth warning of political and economic change that was imposed on us from a single source, a potential leader out of militant Islamic thinking out of the past, Osama (Usama) bin Laden. It was this weak spot in the dike of human events that was ruptured in the New York World Trade Center (WTC) bombings. There were little clues our leaders of the last decade of the millennium who did not understand or relate to until we viewed the world's similarity of events to this dynamic event. Oliver North had been threatened by bin Laden about 1986 and devised a strong electronic security system for his family.

We began to see the pattern, the challenge of dissidents to the Capitalistic freedom loving way of life after the WTC disaster. This manuscript is the author's history of similar trends and events projected by use of cycles for the next decade and hopefully for the next millennium. This is a work interpreting the future based on the past using repeating exogenous cycles that dominate our decision making process.

Wars begin as diversionary moves by the enemy to confuse us and to divert resources and manpower away from their real target. The objective is hidden behind political talk, propaganda and false maneuvers. This confuses us. Should the enemy succeed in gaining confusion and misapplication of our military forces, then another attempt will be made perhaps at the *real* target or another diversion to split our forces making us more vulnerable. If he can force America to spread out thinly then an attempt at the real target may come quickly. We could lose the war before we discern the real intent, if our leadership falters and panics.

The *real* target of the WTC action is to weaken our resolve to act against the Al Qeada and Taliban, which is representing the Islam hate program to destroy America by introducing fear and low morale. When the American public is hamstrung, Islam sleeper plants around the nation, and in Europe, can act to take out our communications, utility systems, power plants and water supplies by sabotage. The crusaders, who visited the Holy Land as Christian protectors, like Islamic people visit Mecca, left behind a lot of destroyed Mosques and dead warriors beginning in the twelfth century. Retribution again.

We have no alternative but to take out this enemy which is the Islam Jihad or become the "has been" nation of the west. Who backs them with money? Saudi Arabia, Iran, Iraq, Palestine and the little nations like Afghanistan, Yemen, Somalia, Egypt, Libya all aided and abetted by the Chinese. Perhaps Pakistan, and Indonesia support their war but not likely.

If you notice, these are the primary petroleum producers of the world. We have a two-front war now: the home front with liberals and fifth columns and with the Islamic nations. Holy wars are the worst because they are illogical, emotional mass actions. It won't be a nice little war.

It all began when Muhammad introduced the Koran to force his religion on his people. Islam means to submit to Allah's (God's) will. The religion is a state religion, in many countries, run by the clerics who make the rules. The current resurgence is fueled by petroleum dollars and planned to retake all lands and nations who oppose their Islamic rule. Only 500 years ago they dominated the Mediterranean lands and Spain.

Preface

Crash is an explanation of why our governments often fail to relieve the economic malaise that periodically occurs following the good times when the "living was easy." Our Constitution encourages corrective action after the debates over problems have been made and legislation written to correct a situation, not to change the course of our society with a special interest agenda.

Their puny attempts to relieve the unemployment, homelessness, drought effects and climate change, or attempts to limit the excesses of industrial activity are painfully laughable for they fail to understand the cause. It is like fighting a typhoon, tide, upheaval or hurricane sweeping the seas, lands, atmosphere and coasts. Not knowing their causes, the battle will only be a token of information and misinformation over the airwaves giving safety precautions for those who seem to be in harm's way. Included here are some cycle explanations.

Presidents take credit for the good times during their tenure of office and blame the bad economic and social events on the "other guys." The legislation writers are usually lawyers, not statesmen and are not even fair in writing legislation, frequently called "pork." These legislative pieces only aggravate the conditions.

Many of these legislators insert clauses in laws for their legal interpretation of future cases of their trial lawyer corporation or for other trial lawyers who contributed to a candidate's campaign.

Constituents and corporations support candidates because they have needs for laws with special clauses giving them hidden advantages. Recommendation: Campaign contributions should be banned or severely limited when from corporation or special interest groups writing the legislation. Elected representatives should be restrained from writing such legislation for any of their constituents if the contribution was in excess of $10,000. It's a tough call, but this is where the problem begins. It is a hangover from our past, the albatross and Gordian knot to be cut by the new leader.

Economics, work cultures, weather and social events (these are synergistic and together alter our view of what is valid, reality) occur in short-term time periods of four, eight, nine and a half, 11, 15, 18-1/2 years, 37 and 55 years. Summary cycles repeat for over 20 and into 55 to 56 years and often, over lifetimes into the 100 and 108-year periods.

Such 18-year cycle events may synchronize by rising in three phases to produce a greater period of prosperity much as did the move from the 1970 lows to 1999 (see 1915 and 1860 similarly) market highs rising in two full waves and one half of the third wave for 29 years of the 37-year cycle.

Then follows the economic and market 2000 blow-off top as earnings reports were released into August 2000. Once we rolled over the market top, the perspective then is to make their probable final bottoms within a major depression stock market and economic low as is projected for late 2007-8. It's like Humpty Dumpty falling off the wall, getting smashed. Will the FRB be able to fix it? It cannot! The FRB tracks the economic cycles. They are not creative leaders.

A more severe crash than usual follows with immense wealth destruction after the rally year 2002-3 occurs, as great social unrest will now spring like unabated weeds in the garden. The WTC Crash came when we were financially most vulnerable, uninformed of the potential damage waiting to be wrought somewhere in our economic and social structure. Proud talk will not alter history.

It is out of the central focus of the most active region or segment of government that the rupture of our life style begins. In this case, it was New York where world trading was centered, on the south end of the island called Manhattan. Like a stick under steady bending stress, it eventually snaps and fractures to destroy itself. So, we must alter our direction, set in a new order of social values to move in a more productive manner or decline into more crashes. Argentina, Afghanistan,

Pakistan, Iraq, Palestine and much of Africa is hanging by a weakening thread in this age.

We will begin to rebuild our society again, and devise new ways to educate the next generation scuttling the teacher unions, much state and Federal bureaucracy, the textbook writer monopoly, increase our high tech economic productivity skills, then venture into new thoughts and philosophies of what life is all about. Perhaps religious wars will destroy many vain protagonists.

This review of projected national societal and economic events is based on the dominant and long-term periodic, a) 18.5-year (9.3-year half wave to the peak of growth), b) the 11.1-year weather cycle (5.6 years of warming, into summer 2000, with less rain and then 5.6-years of cooling and increasing rains into winter 2006) proven with tree ring growth, c) the 22.2-year double sunspot "hot dry" period (note year 2000 as the top) then "cold wet" weather cycle for 11.1 years (average), d) the Presidential Cycle, a four-year inventory period of two years up then two down, and e) the 15-year period of the El Niño and La Niña latitudinal weather storms. Also, their multiples have merging characteristics.

Each of these cycles when doubled increases the intensity of the doubled cycle low, as well as at the major top. Four becomes eight, 18.5 becomes 37 years, 20 years becomes 40 and triple 18.5 becomes the 55-6-year cycle. The 100-year cycle is 9 x 11.1 years of the sunspot series.

The 18.5-year economic lows are due in 2008-9 for the Crash terminal point, not the stock market lows due in early 2007. At these points, multiple periods synchronize to maximize the crisis of world economics, taxes and government administration. Wars at such points seem inevitable.

It is what happens after this date that will determine whether Capitalism prevails, or whether the Osama (or Usama) bin Laden's Islamic fundamentalism prevails throughout the world. Whether he lives or dies, he encouraged the Islam cleric to begin their move to destroy their only real competitor to their religious thought, Capitalism, not Protestantism, Judaism, Catholicism, Hinduism, et al. Perhaps, this is their answer to the wars with the Knights Templar who searched their lands for the Holy Sepulcher mentioned in the Old Testament and the Holy Grail after Christ's last supper. Much destruction of Mohammedan religious temples was the result of the Crusades in the twelfth century.

Does their Islamic educational system show evidence that their religious culture is superior to any other religion or cultural belief? Only Arabs and their converts follow the rituals and indoctrinated beliefs, subjective beliefs! With the dollar money from natural oil resources they are attempting to resurrect the Muhammad dream of world domination. For some, that is all that matters. Russia also tried to dominate the world along with Hitler/Mussolini. The Huns and every population evolving and exploding out of their homelands, the steppes, have made similar attempts to nationalize the world into their image.

America has not aggressively sought to change the world to fit their ideas, but their success at progress and freedom is often seen as desirable and sought by people who can migrate across our borders legally or illegally.

Russia tried to keep their people inside their borders but they kept circumventing the barriers. We have become the refuge of the impoverished, those hungering for freedom to think and believe what they must reason with, to practice scientific concepts, to expand knowledge and their potential in philosophy and verbal expression. There are those among the refugees who still cannot conceive the meaning of freedom ideas and seek dependency on welfare and government programs.

Rebuilding our society must not yield to ritualistic stereo-like thought, since despotism-like leaders were found in early ages thousands of years ago, in the first millennium, and many still prevail in backwater countries like Afghanistan, east from the Bosporus to the western Pacific. In the days near 700 AD Muhammad gave the nomadic people of the Middle East a more cultured set of laws and values; it unified and uplifted their nomadic tribal civilizations into communities and small nations.

The Saracens ruthlessly pursued their religious beliefs killing all who refused to submit to Islam. They conquered most of the western Mediterranean lands and tried to conquer Europe. Their greatness and cruelty lasted until they left on the run in 1492 when the French armies destroyed the Saracen armies. They retreated from Spain to the safety of Africa and remained divided until recent oil revenues brought new life to their beliefs.

In September 2001 they openly challenged the Capitalist system and other modern cultures, those other than Islam and ancient eastern religions Buddhism, Hinduism, etc. They have challenged our greater economic, scientific, social and political success as measured by our prosperity, creativity and technology. Jealously our system has worked well to increase the quality of life in our lands while their tribalism of thousands of years of inbreeding has failed to produce the prosperity Moslems once enjoyed even a few centuries ago. They were prominent in astronomy, mathematics, commerce and built beautiful Moslem religious centers.

Tearing down our society to the level of their current values and by creative leveling is like self-immolation. It is evil! They are self-destructing acts.

Suicide is condemned by all man-devised religions. Somehow, murder for the non-believers in Allah as practiced by fundamental Moslems is anathema to being creative and socially acceptable. Perhaps the heinous practices are merely tools of power, not of the religion. We may never know. Any religion that kills non-believers would seem to be flawed, especially when the controlling clerics energize hatred towards other beliefs.

This use of Islamic law and culture tends to thwart creative and freedom-thinking peoples from evaluating and then implementing social law of our mutual God. The message to take charge of the earth, to discover, populate and be creative seems to be distorted. The failure of a religion to progress their believers over 1300 years suggests there is something wrong with Islam. Overindulgence in rituals over-controls creative new ideas.

We must keep our potential option goal of traveling to another world through the heavens using magnetic pulse engines energized by the magnetic fields in the solar system, even though our religious past wants to keep us from even accepting the thought. Islam would rub out western culture at the expense of all civilized nations if they could but gain sway over their historical tribes and oil producers of the Arab world.

Having discovered the secret of pulse engine magnetic induction for powering our vehicles on land, sea and in space, it is unlikely that oil dominance will last more than another decade. This reduces the fear from Islamic destruction practices as found in their Osama bin Laden leaders. This may have been the last chance when Islam and Arabic ventures could have succeeded.

Perhaps Islam believers feel they have missed the most recent 200 years of prosperity after the western culture closed down the Barbary Pirates and the Moslem population began to recede from the western Mediterranean lands after their defeat in Spain.

Then after WW II the lands of the Arabian Peninsula and Middle East under British Mandate were divided mainly among chiefdoms, nomad strong men, religious philosophies and dominant leaders of the roaming populations. They were given mandated lands to develop as they could.

There is a ritualistic cry today for "getting their share." The only problem is that "their share" is now held by a few rich families who control the oil and their country, like Saddam Hussein of Iraq, Saudi Arabian King Faud, and the lands surrounding Syria, Jordan and Iran. Oil money has been bountiful for a few. Illiterate and narrowly educated people living off the lands and desert sands of homelands get little from the oil sheiks. Their struggle is to gain their share. Certainly, the U.S. does not control their world. The U.S. has been an oil victim, too, since the 1970's.

It is reported that most of the Islamic Mosques built in the U.S. in the past 30 years were funded by the Saudi's to maintain their authority against the rising cry of Islamic clerics who control the schools and preach hatred for American Capitalism. This is a keg of dynamite sitting on the front portico of the White House and with the Saudis in their mosques. We choose to ignore the warning hoping to get ready or until we find another energy solution to propel our vehicles without dependence on Arab oil producers. We are almost there. It will be a close race.

There remains a fifth column in the American culture because the hatred for Capitalism's success is taught in Islam's clerical schools in America also. No matter how apologizing their speakers appear to press on us, their schools are not for religious freedom. Theirs is not for our freedom of religion and Constitutional Law concepts as opposed to Islamic or Catholic or other state religions older even than Christianity.

Those Arab refugees who have been delivered to our lands have likely been duped into thinking they could again achieve Arabian cultural greatness and go to heaven as they are taught in their schools, by osmosis by just living in America.

They do not appear to be capable of or interested in leaving their past behind them and adapting to American freedoms of thinking and to become American-Arabians, eschewing values of self-sufficiency, non-religious indoctrination and control, going for public education instead of religious cleric schools, accepting the Constitution, etc. These immigrants may give us great political and social indigestion in the next few hundred years, much as is the Latino based immigrant culture and others overrunning our cities and trashing our historical values. Diversity is too often an alibi for not Americanizing one's new residents. Diversity remains suspect. The major problem areas being affected follow.

1

When Are Taxes Too Much?

Tax rates have become excessive when reaching over 42%, and history tells us that at this point a culture and level of society has ended. It does take a few years for the glue of society to weaken, but when challenged either breaks-down or rejuvenates.

You've wondered what was happening in the stock markets, the symbols of Capitalism, this past decade and the American economy, and about why the battle looms with Islam's culture versus Capitalism's. This tax rate excess has been in effect for over ten years. (Pessimism may prevail into 2010).

With the high cost of energy, gasoline and natural gas loaded onto the current tax rates, our tax burden just jumped to over 60% at year-end 2000. Add increased transport and operating costs of processing from energy inputs, as add-on premiums to merchandise and you will see the big inflation monster reappear. Surcharges are applied to everything now. Will these charges be rescinded when oil falls again to $10.00 per barrel? In the past, oil profits have been retained by marketers. Does history not repeat? It is up to President George W. Bush to cut the cost of the government programs and free capital for renewed growth.

Deterioration of the western economy is here, and also, overseas. It will resume its degeneration after the big market high due in 2002, in the markets and economy, and politically into late 2002. Until the economy and government breaks down, unable to enforce its own laws

1

and protect the Constitution, or overseas interests in their own corporate and private zones, government may fail to withstand the Islamic onslaught? Dictators usually prevail over failing, weakened morally, economies. The public suffers while dictators build mansions to their reign. This hasn't changed throughout time.

It's much like when the first frost and freeze appears in the autumn. Then everything goes into hibernation, until the spring warmth from direct sunlight and the rains reappear. No matter how hard we try, little growth develops, unless soil temperatures reach above 45° and adequate moisture with sunshine are present. Then nature takes over regardless of what we add as fertilizer to make it productive and happy.

A new era begins perhaps in some other region or culture of the world once the crash and destruction of our crumbling institutions is complete. Some cataclysms may make a recovery, a long-term event requiring many new generations to re-establish their objectivity and creativities.

Until and unless political and economic leaders and the public regain control of their tax system, along with their bureaucratic controls, government's elected and appointed officers, the angry bear economy and stock markets will worsen for many more years.

There is now a negative incentive in the land to invest as in bear or recessive markets and in real estate or equities. Housing starts are falling as in every other 18-year cycle of record. The 37th-year low is usually the point when recovery in housing prices is most noticeable. That date is scheduled as the second 37th-year low, from spring 1933, (1970 also), into spring 2007.

Such deterioration of the economies and social mores are usually found worldwide confirming the degeneration of cultural and the economic values we have known. These values had made this civilization great.

Today, they are being subverted. It seems to be in the minds of a 37-year generation bulge, mainly the boomers, around the world. How or why they were infected with such strange and degenerative ideas is something for historians to analyze. Perhaps it was from the heat of the maximum 26,000-year cycle when man became overwhelmed by exogenous forces. It's happened before.

When rogue nations and corporate alliances can manipulate the price of energy at will, sack our financial institutions with threats of violence and possible nuclear vandalism, we no longer control our destiny.

When the UN can dictate what our social and economic policies will be and force us to pay fees into their organization coffers to destroy ourselves, we have lost our nation and our freedoms. The tobacco settlement is a case in point.

When we will not defend our borders against overwhelming undocumented illegal immigration, we cannot for much longer stand as a free and independent nation. The free movement of revolutionaries through our borders to effect hijacking of our airliners to create manually controlled flying missiles into the WTC spires is a case in point.

We are being tied down, as did the Lilliputians (6 inch tall) in Jonathon Swift's novel "Gulliver's Travels," to the giant (5-½-feet tall) who slept peacefully on their beach recovering from his shipwreck. WTO and the UN treaties are cases in point.

When will we awaken? Will we open our eyes and realize what has happened only when some new government or President suspends our Constitution? Can we save ourselves and remain free? Can the western free market with its personal freedoms be reworked and rebuilt with lowered tax rates, less government and bureaucratic control? Was the crash and destruction in New York and Washington enough to energize us to realize how foolish we have been, fiddling while New York burned? Are these riots we have been experiencing in the past ten years not evidence of a dangerous element in society seeking power for themselves?

Will we be able to save ourselves from the vandals of the world jealously tying our minds with restraints, obligations, regulations, stacked judiciary, international giveaways to plunder our economic power for other nations through OPEC organizations, the UN, by agreements like NAFTA, WTO, leased old military bases by Chinese military organizations in Long Beach, the Panama Canal, the Bahamas, in the Mojave Desert, the central California valley and others and ballistic missile agreements, etc.?

On January 28, 2002, bankrupt Global Crossing announced a $750 million investment by Hutchison Whampoa and Singapore Technologies Telemedia. The Hutchison Whampoa is owned by the Chinese military and operates the above noted bases for China, according to the AP (Associated Press).

In October 2001 the Sinn Fein's Gerry Adams of the Irish Republican Army, hinted it may be willing to give up some of its arms to gain peace in their land. What does this mean? Is this a beginning of the terrorist collapse? Perhaps it is a pause before resuming fierce nationalism.

China, OPEC, Africa and third world nations, Iran, Iraq, Libya, Mexico, India, Pakistan and other small economic nations have a voting plurality in the UN and on legislative commissions such as the WHO, WLO, NAFTA, NATO and many UN agencies.

They have taken over many of our National Parks and lands in the name of world historical monuments. We have lost our destiny, or, perhaps it has been being given away by our socialist leaders. Many of our elected officials have allegiance to other social philosophies, cultures and nations and not to our own Constitution and our national interests. Are we to be swallowed up by the UN? Will we go down by the terrorists destroying western culture? Will they destroy our confidence in our future?

Who can be productive and creative when there is little cash flowing from consumers into buying products so that entrepreneurs can profit too? Is making a profit such a bad idea and word?

Yes, it is among communists and socialists! Could we be facing economic and social stagnation? Could we be destroyed by sabotage from within by cells of anarchists and perhaps Islamic fundamentalists bent on suicidal destruction missions?

There is little incentive beyond survival minimums to work and be creative today, when the majority of profit/cash flows to the government as taxes in one form or another. Redistribution has become a parasite on the creative producers of wealth. Once there is no incentive to start a new business or go through the lengthy bureaucratic procedures to get a patent or copyright, then we do have a serious problem facing the nation's next leaders.

Supporting the bureaucracy is wasted money since they contribute nothing to production or Gross National Product. They have in fact become our managers, not producers.

If President George W. Bush, 43rd President, can lower the tax rates sufficiently, we may be able to avoid the ultimate pain to the American and western culture. European nations have similar risks. Asian, African, South American, and North American nations often follow the nihilistic degradation practice with the over-taxation rule as well. Can the inevitable historical precedent be derailed? Bush managed about a 1% drop in 2001.

With the anti-terrorist war we may be forced to raise taxes again. Liberals would vote for it. Will President Bush be able to prevent the tax increases? Will this accelerate the collapse? As a new tax to support the failing Postal Service with Federal Bill 602P proposed to Congress, a 5¢ surcharge per email delivered in lieu of postage, in addition, a $20 to $40 monthly surcharge for using the Internet would be imposed. This bill would kill the computer and service industry as well as limit world communications. This is a form of censorship!

In past ages once economic and social revolutions occurred deposing kings and potentates, perhaps like French King Louis the Fourteenth who lost his head along with the tax collectors, and friends-of-the-court. The king's royal family and court hangers-on were also beheaded in the French Revolution. Then the worst is over because the continuity of a regime is gone. The rebuilding must follow and not have the culture pillaged and burned. There are always survivors who must begin to rebuild a society.

If populations are still vigorous, disciplined, trained, educated and growing, a recovery can occur. If this new leadership fails to correct the inequities of high taxes and over-regulation, liberal socialistic deals with other nations, then accelerated social and economic deterioration is to be expected.

If the infringements on our Constitution and foreign entanglements can be stopped and repaired, and we have the vigor to refuse to succumb to their looting through our tax system and the Treasury, running major wars with lukewarm allies, then we may find a new hope and rejuvenation of the America that our forefathers built. We have been squandering our heritage much like every third generation seems to do among wealthy or famous families.

The lowered cost of operating government and big social spending programs soon may give grace to the remaining leadership, bureaucrats and the populace that there is still hope for their children's future and our legacy of freedoms.

The lethargy among our elected officials of both major parties and their refusal to alter their goals and practices has the American voter discouraged and is non-voting for their continued attempts to implement programs that are pure waste boondoggles.

Until Washington's "do-nothing but talk and payoff big corporate campaign contributors to Congressional leaders with favorable legislation" is changed, we will continue to decline into cultural and economic stagnation.

The media must also change. The great shakeout in the next eight to ten years is needed to clear our nation of the rascals who feel privileged to harass the public's freedom of expression.

It took a 70-year liberal agenda to reach the current stage of economic strangulation and inept bankrupt educational ideas.

Political Correctness (PC) was common in Greek and Roman times as it is today in western society. It may take 35 more years to begin to eliminate PC, returning to normal or some other extreme thinking of the mass psychology that ebbs and flows. There is much evidence that the alpha part is at work when President Bush squeaked through the barrage of socialistic, political and news nonsense to become our 43rd President.

Economic and social revolutions usually follow sharp increases in taxation, especially when taxes already exceed the 42% level. Our next involvement in war was thrust on us in the September 11, 2001 sabotage of the World Trade Towers in our largest city, New York. This incident struck our homeland!

This first threat occurred in early 1993 when President Clinton, 42nd President, created the greatest tax increase in the nation's history and then backdated it to the beginning of the same year.

Tax collectors have never been popular. Neither have kings and potentates who forced tax collections beyond the 42% level of incomes. Louis the Fourteenth lost his head over the issue. Marie Antoinette was reported to "Let them eat cake" when the peasants complained they had no bread to eat. She went to the block too.

How well a revolution can be contained depends on whether the public has been thoroughly disarmed by its police agencies or the military, and how quickly the newly elected and/or appointed leaders are able to bring down the tax rate and collection procedures to tolerable levels, thereby defusing the crisis.

Many commentators today speak of a revolution against the tax and control of the citizens to wipe out the current offenders of our liberty. The revolution must be through election of responsible leaders who seek to eliminate the growth and taxation of big government.

President Clinton stated "The era of big government is over." He then promptly began filling his cabinet with countless new bureaucratic programs and staffed them with liberals from ecologists to spin doctors. Such puffery by politicians must be considered buffoonery, not political leadership and campaign rhetoric. We must judge the leader more on what he does than what he says he plans to do. More governors with a record that is compatible to the national and world needs should be elected and fewer with hopes for changing the world.

The world will change the economy and the programs we aspire if we do not guide our leaders by supporting them with good congressional thinkers.

Thorsten Veblen, a Stanford University economics educator and historian, researched the great nations of history to determine at what tax level their cultural demise began. It was 42%. And, we are now looking at 60% in just a few short years of creeping government and energy tax and cost pricing.

The U.S. of A. is well above that critical level and in some calculations, excludes hidden double-taxation. It is closer to 50%, above that critical level as we turn into the third millennium AD. In Sweden and France the critical level was exceeded long ago, and they now have stagnant economies. They know socialism doesn't work, but they have no way out without some sort of revolutionary act that destroys government and its liabilities for the public services. The public fears the risk to their privilege and retirement as well as their lives. They have paid a dear price for their wars still in recent memory.

There are few crises for this first decade that will dominate the nation's economy more than the Crash that is expected to extend into 2008-10. As in the World Trade Towers, the evil symptoms are thought of as the Islam revolutionaries. They remain oil-funded destroyers in the name of religion, funded with our dollars.

Headaches usually are minor, but when temperatures rise, a new wave of possibilities is encountered by the doctor and patient alike. Add other symptoms and soon the consultation fees become extended into new areas of research. The doctors' conclusions may be challenged for years. The patient may die long before a diagnosis is made and a cure suggested. We are in that state of the economy today. What is the disease? What is the cure?

Let us review some of them before we get into some specific economic, market and social conditions that will likely prevail into 2010, ending the first decade of this millennium. Some economists are beginning to realize the patient may die before a cure is found.

Still they have no new theory of economics other than the one John Maynard Keynes proposed and President Roosevelt accepted before the facts were exposed to tests of validity. We ran out of time after nearly 70-years of manipulating money supply, interest rates and using pump-priming methods, using make-work programs, etc before the system broke down.

Economic and social events tend to follow the primary market/economic cycle delivering the issue that is to prevail into the final peak. Then, the correction phase follows into the terminal crisis to wipeouts of unprepared businessmen and employees. The public at large is psyched-out to retract their spending, investing, traveling, building, and even logical thinking. New city councils regress in their practices undoing much of their predecessors' good. They fractionalize their objectivity and become little fiefdoms intent on building their personal careers instead of showing leadership for the good of the community. It progresses into the larger cities, states, regional activities and the nation.

In the end, it is in creating through all the nations of the world, building better programs of governing than were developed by earlier leaders. This degenerates in longer time spans into survival programs blocking outsiders from participating in a community's activities. We regress to earlier times of trading/ bartering as some currencies become worthless. It is as true in Europe today with hard versus soft currencies as in many cities of the world. The Euro has destroyed all the cultural baggage nations have been proud of in their coins and paper. Gold has disappeared except for bullion.

Its resolution is partly in our hands, but mainly within the culture's current pattern of technological evolution. Unchecked, the cycle either destroys or rejuvenates. It rejuvenates when we establish a plan and implement it when the dominant (18 and 20-year) recessive cycle ends.

Being aware of the problems today, society can minimize the dominant cycle's effects modestly or severely depending on how strong our leaders try and the public cooperates. Left to drift we will follow the slippery slope into history as a "has-been" culture and nation. With good leaders our risks can be limited. We can plan ahead preparing for the day new technology is ready and the cycles are due to resume new growth.

Once the cycle bottom has been reached, we can plan to take advantage of the next nine-year upswing of the 18.5-year cycle low into 2019 in economic matters to prosper again. Will the recovery be possible? Should the recovery period only give the economy minor results, to say 50% of the previous nine-year decline, more severe cutbacks will surely follow as the economy shrinks into anarchy.

We must remain aware that a 20-year cycle persists and is due to bottom about that same time frame. This may give us a flat recovery period into 2019-20 before all the issues are focused on rebuilding our nation in the western world. The eastern lands and Middle-East where the violence seems to persist should be given help in solving their heritage problems. Leaders must change and the future improved for populations with differing cultural beliefs and who are teaching hate America and hate Capitalism in their religious schools. There are few public schools in the regions, which leaves the Islam and more ancient religions in the teaching business prolonging the rituals that seem to be holding back the minds of the students, keeping them from perceiving a better way.

If our President and administrative leaders have done their job well and the Congressional leaders have given political aspirations a more meaningful look, then we may be able to thwart history's record of major crashes and then recovery. Investors are used to buying in the stock market dips thinking the next recovery is just weeks away. We do not realize that the precipice we are now facing is more than just a blip in time that, possibly, the major trend has turned against our culture and Capitalism.

Politically, the liberal Democratic element still dominates much of the legislative agenda. It could become excited and readily blame the

Republican President Bush in the 2002 election by taking over the House or gaining more Senators.

It does not seem to be likely for this to occur except that off year elections often produce a loss of seats and may reverse the power structure. With the plurality of trust in George W. Bush as our President and his cabinet of effective administrators, Congress remains the only problem. Bush approval ratings have been running 85-90%, highest for any president of record.

The war is expected to last into 2008 as numerous terrorist organizations and nations find their funds cut off, their leaders imprisoned and restraints place on their expenditures for weapons of mass destruction. It is the battle to save the civilization we have built over several thousands of years. Note that this date is near the terminal extreme lows of the 18.5-year cycle. As the battles are won, the worst will likely be in 2008.

Again, in 2004 at the four-year economic and market lows, they could be emboldened for this is when the natural four-year cycle recession low occurs. Their attempt may backfire since the trend has turned sharply into more conservative ideas and lifestyles.

Many think of "liberals" as Democrats in social philosophy. They are not of the same ilk. Liberals have a socialistic bias and think through a screen of idea words that are interpreted as a different role for government, not one for the people to decide. Democrats in general are more of an opposing power group who want to run government programs to control the voter at election time to maintain control of the power structure.

Republican ideas are that the voter should manage his own affairs with as little help from government as possible. This is their kind of referendum on what is important. This is the ying-yang swing found in all historical programs of all societies. We are repeating a long long-term phase.

Liberals are preparing to pounce upon the Bush Administration and to break the back of this half-warm Republican coalition delicately balanced in Congress. The state legislatures are doing well as are Republican Governors. Will the Republican philosophical edge falter? What if they blink in the next crisis? Can the Senate be governed with just a one-vote majority by the liberal senate leader Tom Daschle, or some other newly elected liberal?

So far, President Bush (43rd) has taken a strong leadership role. The voters' approval is well over 85% supporting Bush's programs and the war, the greatest reported found in history. So, it looks like a sound policy change may deliver political and economic change.

Let us look at the key to this dilemma, the California voters. Still they are only 15% liberal and Democratic while 26% are Republican and many are retired from work rolls. With 51% registered Independent they swing with their personal prosperity and who like to vote on initiatives to tell the legislature what it must do when they don't do it right. They are volatile.

This does not count the 10% who vote for Libertarian candidates, socialist and other political persuasions. Can these voters be trusted to "throw out the bums" in 2002 elections? How about 2004? Then 2008?

The energy crisis is just the effect of a negative and manipulative leadership thinking, which has prevailed for the past 30 years. Squandering the tax over-payments with the energy crisis paying too much for the energy merchandise, for political purposes, probably will bring the liberal administration to its knees. We think they will buckle under the confused Gray Davis leadership in power prior to 2002.

What an awful political conflict the state of California possesses, when Democratic leaders refuse to do their job right for nearly 30 years. Add the floating Latino population and the mostly undocumented immigrant population that is trying to take over California and the southwest again and you can visualize street battles, vicious politics and economic troubles ahead.

Our battles are not likely from the Al Qaeda (the base) for Afghanistan terrorists and Osama bin Laden, the leader who hates America for his own reasons, but from the Hispanic and black gangs taking advantage of the limited military and police services spread thin to protect our major cities.

Riots are a new tool around the world. December 2001 saw major attempts to overrun the guards for the Channel in an attempt to get to England where liberal laws for refugees and homeless give them an advantage. They were caught and blocked from walking the 33 miles under the English Channel.

Interference from President Vicente Fox (de Mexico) into the boiling cauldron attempting to empower "illegals" will become a major issue before the elections of 2008 and turn the crisis into a nightmare. He is attempting to set the agenda so that he will be able to control the actions of U.S. Congress. In a deal with the Governor Gray Davis in 2001 he received privileges for his nationals to gain subsidized access to the State University system should those who spent three years in California high schools apply.

Still the liberal Democrats try to bring in more "illegals" and make them into Democratic voters during election days. "Win the election at any cost" politics could become the start of the new revolution we struggle to avoid by getting out the legally registered voters at elections. President Bush hopes to capture these same undocumented voters in the next series of elections. They are still not legal residents. We are our own worst enemy trying to win these elections. The vice is here. Too many legal organizations support these undocumented and fight our immigration policy, what little is still enforced.

Sometimes the taxing authority, other than the government income taxes or excise taxes on imports and exports, turns out to be a business monopoly controlling a major element of our economy necessary to maintain our life styles, e.g. energy, a scarce mineral, labor unions or even, skilled populations needed to build products for our own defense. State dictators often create such monopolies for their domestic products and own corporate shares.

Tax rates modify the cycle of achievements and the greatness of any nation. When taxes of all entities within a nation reach above 42% of the gross income of its working nationals, the nation begins a decline like when the organism is infected with a parasite or cancer eating its guts, depleting its energy until a vital organ becomes infected too. Suddenly, it is too late and rigor mortis shows in the morgue of history.

This figure does not include subsidies to farmers, industry, transportation and foreign corporations, often in foreign nations. Price controls from agricultural groups like milk producers, corn producers who grow crops for extracting energy blending supplements ostensibly to reduce smog output of automobiles, cotton, peanuts, etc. are not included. These price controls are just another tax form that raises prices for a specific segment of our economy. Recent shifting of costs to the Federal government to provide security personnel and equipment to airlines, busses and railroads are not included.

The percent of industry that is given over to government is like loading the deck of a ship so that it is too one-sided or top heavy. The ship may suddenly capsize when a wave strikes it broadside. Was this wave the destruction of the twin towers? We should phase out all these bureaucracies over the next ten years while economic problems are difficult for us all. We could lower our costs of living directly and renew our tax structure at the same time.

The Crash from over-taxation:

Events are sudden and swift disturbing the peace and tranquility of government and its citizens. The cultural demise usually arrives before the public can be aroused. When an incident occurs, they will likely panic. That is why this book was written for you. The media will try to overwhelm the reader/viewer and his rock solid beliefs with propaganda campaigns leading to false hopes and diversions.

Politicians and leaders often fail to act and to act properly, insolated as they are against the whims of voter duress and complaints of heavy tax loads during their tenure.

The signals of the illness of the nation are noticed slowly and occur over long periods of crises, which crises are rarely solved but remain, to debilitate the economy.

Rationalizing the problems and blaming authority figures seldom solve the problems, but it sounds good for the misinformed. They are again the slaughtered goats on the altar of freedom and hope.

It may be a world economy, a type of economy that many nations enfold, or an isolated backward area of tentative prosperity that slowly moves into apathy, but like all diseases and viruses, they cross borders silently much as during the Passover days in ancient Egypt.

2

Tipping the Scales

Tipping scales is an old game practiced by street merchants—weighing the thumb, too.

We have about 29 million adults on the Federal payroll. States show a lesser amount totaling 14.8 million state employees for a total of 43.8 million, not counting subsidized services, welfare programs, grants to subsidize foreign projects and tax funded independent agencies, incarcerated prisoners, etc., per census 2000.

This 43.8-million total of government employees against around 110 million taxpayers (out of a population of 283 million) equals nearly 40% of the tax paying employed (year 2000 census) population. This number (higher paid than most privately employed citizens) is used to manage all of us citizens and non-citizens alike, a cadre of elitists. We have over 16 million of these taxpayers employed who make less than poverty line wages and who do not pay taxes. These are subsidized and should be counted as Federal employees since they receive the benefits of our government, vote and serve in low income jobs they have been adopted as employees. They are hardly paying their way in taxes. Whether the liberal concept of raising minimum wages would reduce their ranks or not, the mandated costs raises the general cost of living. Hence, the public at large pays a premium for their subsidy.

This leaves so few of us to do the production and marketing! The burden in retirement benefits and shortening work-week benefits gets heavier each year. Then there are those public servants who retire early on disability at greater levels than do the fully vested retirees like in the police, fire, contractors and internal government elected. Their cumulative retirement benefits continue to build the premiums for insurance policies.

With 40 % of the taxpayer population (43.8 million) holding public payroll jobs, at average size family of one dependant per adult we have another 43.8 million for a government total of 87.6 million.

Let us add the 12.3% or 34.8 million receiving SSI benefits including the (aid to) dependants of deceased taxpayers, the ill or in prison are about 4% today for 4.1 million, 4% unemployed for 4.11 million some being retrained under federal subsidy programs, we total another 43 million more people receiving direct income from government. (See how important SSI votes are in any election?)

Our unemployment rate in autumn of 2001 was around 4%, supported by industry paying compensation much as a tax—that is, about 4.11-million receiving benefits,

The grand total of employees and dependants in government jobs at 87.6 million plus 34.8 million for SSI, plus 4.1 million for indigent and prisoners, plus 4.1 million receiving unemployment insurance we reach 130.6 million or 46.15% of the total population receiving benefits from governments. This total does not count benefits paid for welfare, aid to dependant children, food stamps, WIC and make work programs of various government agencies.

We have made no calculations for the contractors given preference because of sex, color, race and refugee status privileges being subsidized with higher valuations for contracts, also subsidy for housing, food, or make-work jobs with low cost housing. Direct subsidies to family farms, corporate farms, farm products sold or given to foreign nations where crops were bought by the Agriculture Department are not counted as costs, but they are and raise the inflation rate by holding prices up.

With 53.85% non-government employed or 152.4 million self-employed supporting taxpayers/dependants working in private industry, or 169.8 million, that leaves us close to the breakeven point. This is in excess of the 42-58% balance noted by our researcher being close to the 46.2-53.8% close to tipping over point noted by our Stanford researcher as the breaking point, only in terms of population instead of taxes. Maybe the average worker 9-to-5 or 6-2 shift doesn't worry about this, but any good economist would begin to look for a good government job until he could retire. We know that corporations pay most of the taxes and stockholders are double taxed for their share-holder dividends and capital gains. Perhaps this lack of dividends is the hole in the bucket that loses the corporate profits.

How long can the non-public workers, the private economy, support the burden of our government managers? The numbers still increase every year, not counting consultants and contract service providers used intermittently as needs change.

The tax burden or wave is another hidden disaster, waiting for a tsunami-like impact broadside to the nation. It may be triggered by a pestilence, disease, agricultural failure, drug disabilities and dissipation, a war, a wayward or rogue missile, an energy shortfall crisis, an invasion or sabotaging of our nation by planting infectious diseases like small pox, anthrax, bombs, germ warfare plants or a similar powerful force that knocks the nation off balance throwing normal marketing channels into the ditch.

Government bailouts and rebuilding programs can exhaust the remainder of the non-government employee' disposable resources, dropping the available tax funds, but increasing the need for raising tax loads to cover shortfalls. Government needs seem endless as they constantly search for new tax bites where the taxpayer doesn't look—raising water, trash and sewer fees, telephone fees, internet fees (?), hidden taxes on Real Estate sales, auto sales, and when you are too busy to notice, places where they add charges to your taxes. Very often, the tax is imposed on corporations, which hides the tax thereby passing it along to the consumer in higher prices.

For the doubting Thomas (biblical, not from Missouri) here is a partial list of great empires we know of that have come and gone having reached over the magical 42% level: Roman, Greek, Alexander the Great, Ottoman, Turk, Mongol, (Genghis) Kahn, British, Dutch, Portuguese, Russian, Spanish (which claimed most of western hemisphere once), Third Reich. The Arabs in the seventh century once circled the Mediterranean lands. And, the Chinese emperors known back to 4000 BC, in their times, ran the known civilized world. Great civilizations have had their times in the spotlight! The Japanese seem to have avoided this list, so far. It is deteriorating rapidly and is vulnerable to N. Korean attack. But it has been suggested that they may slip into history as economic powerhouses within the next 20 years.

In Asia and Mexico archaeologists are still uncovering evidence of civilizations and cultures productive and dominant over 6000 years ago. Some are suspected of being active over 10,000 years ago.

Evidence of Atlantis' culture of ancient times may have been found recently in the seas covered by 2200 feet of the Atlantic Ocean between Cuba and Bimini and the islands within the Bermuda Triangle. Some researchers suggest a land rising may bring the old land into the world culture again by mid-century.

Some refer to the SE Mexican coast as the site of Atlantis, while others speak of the region known today as the Antarctic.

The wind blows against every age and culture trying with its power to subdue the civilized forces man has created. Can we survive this attempt by nature to replace our system, or will we succumb to the historical pattern now that western civilization has been brought to the brink?

3

Free Money is Never Free

The freedom to engage in enterprise using capital markets to leverage funding does make the capitalism game the great opportunity for an idea, hopefully to become a mass service movement and perhaps a profitable operation for many investors.

Capital raising economies create prosperity by employing savings from participating citizens. Of course, to participate, one's income must be greater than the immediate need to survive and funds must not be needed for daily survival, and could be lost completely.

More winners than losers have made the Capitalistic System a success around the world. A steady dollar-investment averaging program will produce lower than average stock cost positions in major corporations. The corporations continue to grow, just like plants and animals in agriculture and animal husbandry.

With a steady dividend or corporate growth pattern, great retirement and personal living benefits continue to accrue, the system expands giving prosperity to greater numbers. Starting your own business with OPM (Other Peoples Money) is even better for people with creative ideas and ability to manage ideas and the performance of others. The leverage gained is a great plus.

It also allows one to become a failure, to start over with more experience, to go forward to try again. This is one thing that has made America great, and the access to capital allowed us to pursue the dream.

4

Importance of Cycles

Cycles are a revived scientific idea. They have always been with us and have manipulated our lives in ways we hardly recognize.

Corporate earnings usually lag up to six months tracking the individual cycles because of accounting and shipping procedures. The economic cycle peak often appears six months (two quarters) after the two-year high, or at the 30th month, the mid-point or second year of the four-year cycle. This confuses many who analyze data. This lag event is an accounting problem. The cycle is still there. All we need to do is recognize the cycle and the point of change in direction of the effects. Corporate accounting that is quarterly shows the data delayed in their earnings reports. If the cycle ends near their quarterly closing report there may be only a quarter lag. But if the report is at the fifth or fourth month of the quarterly business cycle, accounting may show the turns early or off nearly six months for the majority of reports.

If corporations could use such non-quarterly reports, we might get an earlier signal of a reversal and prosper from being better prepared. Earnings also lag after the peak of the 18.5-year cycle by about six months. Because these earnings reports occur in the final days of the 18-year cycle, the "fundamental investor" often sells into this low on the bad news. The CPA analysis may prove to be premature or misleading at major tops and bottoms.

Savvy investors sell these terminal market rallies. Likewise, the lag factor in showing an economic recovery in business and government statistics runs about two quarters after the low. The government tends to accumulate data until year-end or perhaps several quarters delayed during the accounting year. This gives the government stats little advance warning, but often confirms the problems since they measure three quarters in a row as confirming a trend change. The lows are found in the financial markets first, then, follow in the quarterly reports. This failure of government reports to guide our industry is no longer acceptable.

Government reports of employment and unemployment always lag about a year because rehired employees are brought in usually some two quarters after the renewed product demand begins and after the use of overtime becomes too difficult to keep the production level equal to the demand. Once business is assured that the economy, the demand for its products is not a fluke or a strange order inflow for unseen reasons, like a war, then it rehires.

After the 11-year (average) sunspot peak and our northern seasons grow cooler, finally into the cycle lows five and one half years later, rains become bountiful in most northern hemisphere seasonal regions. They form as latitudinal strata moving northward, then southward over the lands in eleven and 15-year cycles.

When three of these 18.5-year sequences work together they form the 55.5-year cycle. We drag out the problems because we are now approaching a 60-year cycle low also.

That is, three 15-year weather cycles = 45 while 4 x 15 = 60 years, low to low. To the low dates five 11.1-year cycles = 55.5 years. Three 18.5-year cycles equals 55.5 years. They synchronize, totaling a major low at the 55.5-year low.

The Crash into the lows of 60-year weather cycles and 55.5-year sunspot cycles gives compounded problems and varies like wandering economic events in the desert of life. Now that you know why we get the big crash every 55.5 years and you know when the lows were last recorded, you can pencil in the dates for future four-year events and on into the big lows due in 2008-10.

Cycles are additive as well as deductive, and in the declining phase must be deducted from the total accrual. This deductive period is often called a "consolidation" period by analysts, which may last up to six years. So, we begin to recognize that with the four-year cycle low in 1998 we would get a low in autumn or in winter 2002. Then follows the rally into 2004; followed by the panic crash in 2007-8. The 18-year cycle then is due in late May 2007 to autumn for the financial markets. For the economy it would be two quarters later as renewed consumer interest translates into purchases at retail, reorders flow to factories and the accounting profits lag for the full two quarters into year-end reports.

The 11-year cycle then gives torrential rains in the northern hemisphere in 2006 and tapers back into warm summers in 2011 when the solar max is due. Trees and crops are more fruitful once the rains appear, even with irrigation. Hence tree rings and fruit trees are blessed with alkalinity being purged from the dry years. It should be noted that fisheries are low producers in the coastal and inland waterways when the sunspots are numerous and the rains are less bountiful.

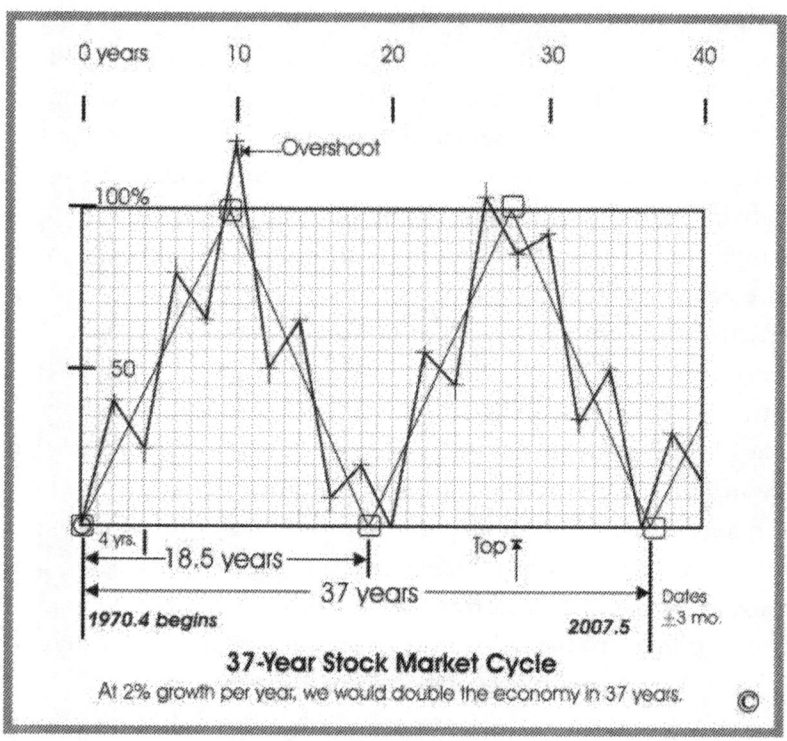

Chart 1

Most of us cannot remember what economic or social events happened last year. But in studying repeating patterns of events and market price changes, there is a pattern of repetition over 55 years, twice the 18.5-year cycle for 37 years and the basic 18-year *generation cycle*. When growth factors and the removal of "hot" stocks and dying companies are rationalized out of the discussion, the actual pattern repeats substantially as it did in previous periods, only with new players. The reason is the cause of much of our life experience and social action is exogenous. It is only because of records kept in the past few hundred years that we are able to discern the repetition. Interest rates and events of 20 years ago also repeat almost to the day.

Chart 1—37-Year Stock Market Cycle

When the salmon run with the early fall rains along the coasts seeking their headwaters upstream, the major fishing cycle will improve. We may want to claim ecological purity for this reason, but when the fish appear even ecologists are surprised. But, when the peak has passed, their fry may show little promise. After years at sea, getting fat on local supplies of food, they will seek again to spawn. Ecologists should prepare their speeches and be ready to pronounce their success at managing the rivers and oceans when they learn the cycle of the fishes. 1991.2 was a good year and 2000.8 (September), then 2010.4, then 2020, then 2029.6 should be bountiful harvest seasons for fishermen. Of course, 2024.8, 2015.2, 2005.6 and 1996 would be poor harvest years. This would make salmon more expensive while at peak harvests the prices would be lower. But, the fishing is the thing, not the price.

This new economic concept explains why we have these economic variations and deviations from statistical averages, as generally applied to technical data.

Too many economists, businessmen and politicians tend to use straight-line projections of two points off a graph to prove their thesis. Such teachings have proven to be traps in logical understanding of life's cyclical events.

Global warming cries turn to global cooling as confusion reigns over weather's cause-to-effect. They are synergistic phenomena linking weather, the economy, prosperity and recession cycles. These are not man-made phenomena. They are only man's reactions to the energy forces surrounding our world. Authorities who comment about ecological matters and then in the next statement blame the cause on a segment of society are, really, very incoherent. They cannot sort the apples from the oranges.

Within these cycles is the four-year cycle, which usually bottoms in spike-down type stock market lows in October every fourth year, often called the Presidential (election) cycle. Analysts call such stocks as those that follow to be cyclical. Some call this the "inventory cycle" since most entrepreneurs become too ambitious near the peak of the cycle, by buying too much inventory stock. The borrowers, consequently, are forced by bankers and suppliers to liquidate into the cycle lows.

Interest rates rise into the peak of their economic cycle. They bottom near lows when bankers begin to agree with the FR Banking system and tighten lending practices until their lows are mutual. Interest rates are the consequence of borrowing by consumers and some business, replicating the economic cycle. Their greed and optimism maximizes at cycle peaks.

In terms of net corporate earnings, these are first reported as strongest, at about the 30th month after the previous major market actual cycle lows. Within some six months following the cycle periodic peak, at the 24th month, corporate earnings peak as accounting and product shipping complete their action stages. That is, from the initial market low plus thirty months for the earnings reports to appear, comes the last of the bad news after the cycle has terminated its downtrend. This is the shift from one end to the beginning the next four-year cycle i.e. Presidential or Inventory.

The newer and fundamental investor often buys on hearing the good news into the 30-month earnings report or top, while the savvy investors sell into the good news at the actual cycle peak i.e. sales, contracts, order peaks, etc. Thus, the market saying "Buy the rumor, sell on the (good) news."

Ah yes, experience counts if one learns the lesson by being a student of human behavior. Eighteen months of stock market and economic decline will teach great lessons in dollar averaging—or planning ahead. When one tends to see sugarplums dancing and carrots preceding the rabbit at stockholder meetings and when CEO's spout drivel, it is time to launch into defensive stocks and bonds.

Stock investors and buyers return when consumers begin to populate and actually buy at retail stores after the dollar sales volume low occurs, with tally reports showing month to month increases for a quarter. Retailers remain reluctant to reorder new product lines until "liquidation sales" clear old merchandise.

Factory orders remain weak until the new season begins, or evidence of a recovery shows in the holiday season's sales. Weaker sales means discounting begins before Christmas and Thanksgiving to clear seasonal inventories. Bargains galore abound like in Christmas 2001!

This is also when the short-term economic events cause layoffs and retailers hold frequent sales to pay their rent. Industry cuts back on labor and material costs to remain solvent. The nine-year cycle gives the peak of the 18.5-year period. It came in late August 2000, two quarters following the cycle peak in spring of 2000. Remember that lesson, the time lag.

It is little wonder, if you allow yourself the integrity to follow the cycle concepts, that the next nine years into 2008 will be most difficult. Depressing stock markets, slow real estate sales and slow construction, slow retail store sales and minor expansion planning, all, naturally, are being held back until the contraction cycle minimums are found near the bottom. The usual extreme numbers will terminate the cycle. Some compare this to a metal spring coiling into compression, followed by the explosion as seen in the market's initial short covering rally when the cycle turns.

Traders sell short mainly into the lows when it seems obvious the market rally is failing. When the majority of the traders get to be psychological bears, it is time for the bulls to ravage them buying the depressed stocks causing the first short covering rally of the new cycle. The figure can be found as when Investment Advisors reach 50% bears or negative on the market, it is time to begin picking up quality stocks and stocks beat down by bad news.

You must know when to expect that low in order to maximize profit. Guessing all the way down to the bottom can break an investor financially. Investor's Intelligence provides that information. It can be found also in Investors Business Daily.

It is during this time, near the bottom, when store modernization should be done. Only when the cycle has reached its terminal bottom will the consumer return to the scene to spend money, businessmen begin to hire new employees, confidence returns, banks begin to lend money (as a result?) and, at cheaper rates, and crops start to improve with better and more timely rains.

Many businessmen modernize stores at the market top when they have more income and paint-up near the slow bottom days cleaning up the neglected appearance and mess.

Mergers come near major tops, bankruptcies occur near major bottoms. Good management should follow the cycles and merge at lows but do stock buybacks in the weakness, when stock prices are their lowest and then liquidate into the flurry at higher price tops.

But, since few know when these final stages are due to appear, they overplay their cards at the opposite cycle extremes. Leading firms, which buy back stock issued near major market lows, are likely to outperform their competitors in the rebuilding of market share during the recovery period. Greed and fear dominate action.

These are the main cycles of greater than 136-days (4.5 months) in time length, which, incidentally, is also a multiple and a fraction of the nine-year cycle period. It is also a multiple of the 68-day periodic swing of the stock markets and earnings. The 90-day cycle has been used primarily in commodities and in banking circles.

Other cycles of shorter and intermediate term importance give some peculiar twists to the economy and weather events. These are events we remember when we visit the family and talk such as the droughts, the big snows, the heavy rains and floods, depressions (when jobs are hard to get) and the prosperous times when we can afford a big vacation or a new car. Near the cycle peak, we buy that new home, take the big vacation, get married with a splurge and invest near the top of the stock market.

The counterpart following prosperity then brings us layoffs, hard times, droughts and confused thinking. We try to find explanations about what causes it all and who is responsible but never find an anchor to confirm causes.

We are only participants in the great natural social programs of life. Man must play out his role in the game of life or life will make him miserable, it will break his spirit and he will blame the system, his company, competitor, the war, the flood, the in-laws, or whatever. They do get very confused at times.

No one is to blame unless laws are written by sharp lawyers making a segment of society more vulnerable to loss or penalty for human events of the times. E.g. bank lending to the officers or friends of the bank, buying futures for inventory at peak prices like Enron, which speculated with futures market procedures before its financial demise in November 2001. There may be insurance company fraud when used to protect certain portions of society but leaving long-term contract policies deflated holding little residual value, with CD and savings depositors paying off the bills, defaults on contracts or mortgages, etc.

For economic failures we usually blame the incompetence of the boss, the banker, the politician, or someone we don't know, certainly not ourselves. We look for a fall guy, a political party, an agency, sometimes a god, a foreign government or a business. Sometimes a nation resorts to a war as a diversion from reality, while at other times a drought persists around the world until food and crops are not available at reasonable prices, then inflation reappears. We all suffer in trying to survive. Cash and credit shortages aid and abet depressions while droughts and doubts cloud our minds. The entire farm program in this nation is twisted and distorted by political groups trying to get subsidies, favorable tax treatment, guaranteed prices for crops and with little concern for the public. We have degenerated into special interest groups buying legislators in state and in Washington to get favorable profits for themselves regardless of what it does to the general economy. Like President Clinton admonished those who could not afford to stay on the farm or in merchandising—"Raise prices!" There was no consideration for foreign price costs or domestic competition as substitute products enter the market for any item.

Few know what causes these things. Scientists refuse to recognize the connections of social and economic events as being related to weather or other forces beyond our control. Those in power will defend their positions until the market and economic collapse occurs. Like a tree in a hurricane that seldom bends will crack long before the waving palm trees lose their fronds. So will the academic defenders of causes, agreed to and taught at the universities, scientists, politicians who get contributions, teachers and union leaders fight until their cause collapses. New leaders will appear and fill the vacuum. It is then we may make great progress and a new cycle begins.

John Maynard Keynes had his theory (1936) accepted in the economic and financial collapse of the Great Depression by President Franklin D. Roosevelt. Keynes' work replaced the mercantilist world concept. The evolutionary change of the industrial revolution after Ricardo in 1817 put politics and taxation into the equation. Then J. S. Mill appeared with valuation theories to compound matters after Ricardo. Along came inflation and deflation, booms and depressions into the 1930's as theory after theory failed or new phenomena displaced the simplicity of the past.

Keynes' theory has been thoroughly disproved for over 30 years. It remains in use because there is no other theory that has been demonstrated to guide our economic and financial planning as industrial and technological nations dominate the next millennium. The void must be filled with a super system and it is believed that system is with the cyclical forces that are the evidence as presented in Crash.

The cause of our current woe is none of those reasons as promoted by the press, academics in and out of government and market analysts measuring values. We rationalize the causes not knowing where the truth might rest. Rationalizing is what the news media seem to specialize in doing, along with politicians and popular economists grasping for a fathomable idea to express their erudition.

Everyone has difficulty understanding economics and so do the professional economists. Few politicians and voters have had a course in economics even with the current (discredited) Keynesian Theory.

Theirs is a professional game of tracking categories of events in the economy by the numbers and then using statistical analysis to try to understand what happened in any given segment of economic and social life. That's called business analysis.

Chairman Alan Greenspan of the FRB (Federal Reserve Board) uses 'time-tested' interest rate and money supply programs and models based on the Keynesian Theory of money supply. Its cost called interest and money (trading) velocity (rate of turnover and spreading among business, jobs, etc.) followed by money supply constitute the stable of tools the FRB has to relieve the depression and recession affects. Sometimes they work well, sometimes not.

Sometimes the FRB finds its methods are no longer effective. This period, at the turn of this third millennium, is one of those times when the economists mill around at their conventions, then grab straws in the verbal winds from suggestions found in the papers being read.

Economists, politicians, consumers and union leaders alike blame NAFTA, WTO, Chinese imports, Mexican imports, OPEC oil prices, and/or environmentalists for restraining energy production, refinery building and energy exploration as current cycle causes. Smog from older generators is often used as the reason environmentalists deny permits for modern energy generators to relieve the shortfalls of our living needs.

These are all effects of cycles, not causes. No one is personally responsible except that the responsible leader should be fully informed that unless there are shenanigans involved, much of the cause is nature at work. We can limit the damage by rain if we just shut the window or put on the tarpaulin.

Big business' monopoly practices, droughts, tropical storms and hurricanes, volcano eruptions, along with earthquakes are being blamed for the cause of our economic problems. We blamed Osama bin Laden for his attacks on our vulnerable society. He is only playing his role as spoiler. It is simply a case of not knowing, or determining objectively what is cause, and what is the effect.

Most news media anchors spend their camera moments on line presenting rationalized incoherent reasoning about the cause of something, but always with the authoritative voice and supporting TV pictures of events illustrating their beliefs. They interpret the human action or reaction as the cause when it is in reality the cycle effect. Human nature is the normal reaction to cyclical forces.

The loss of viewers and newspaper readers is evidence that these media services are not working with the trend of the times. They still seek to impose their ideas on the public believing they are capable of managing the faithful viewers. Advertisers are not getting the results they need so they cancel time contracts. Media blames the consumer, but the consumer may have changed his interests at the turn of this millennium and is going toward more realistic talk radio, reading books and holding conversations on internet, all being oriented toward getting answers and within the current evolving think values. Media is thought to be indoctrinating with their commercial agenda, like Hollywood tries to generate their image of what society should be.

The author spent over 50 years researching these causes and verifying their effects. They constantly recur as cycles and they are found to be just the orderly sequences of life's generational events.

Women's skirts shorten in warmer "good times" periods and lengthen in colder periods and more depressing times. Remember the roaring twenties and the short skirts, with partying, drinking illegal booze and speculating like it was the new way of the world? Maybe you don't remember but the history of the happy times before the crash of '29 engulfed the capitalistic world from central European banks collapsing dragging inter-bank lenders into bankruptcy until it hit New York. At the same time, the Smoot-Hawley tariff act was blamed. It was Roosevelt who closed the banks and Building and Loan bankers that brought the crash home to everyone. There was little money in circulation after that. It is similar to today with Greenspan's highly supplied M1-M2-M3 money supply that has prevented any great collapse at this downturn. Suddenly shrinking M2 and M3 as well as M1 shorter term money could trigger a collapse. Failure to expand money supply as the cycle turns upward would mute much growth time.

Argentina is near collapse financially as well as politically and may compound world economic stability. We are floating in greenbacks, today, and bank liquidity. Interest rates are near Great Depression lows and banks are very reluctant to lend money for incentive construction or business inventories. We have learned some smart financial tactics in the past 80 years. The author is not so sure this is correct, but appears that way. The cycles test all theories and evidence. Synchronize with them or you lose.

By using these repeating events and by knowing when each cycle period begins and ends and when the peaks are due we can take advantage of changes. Then, we can outline the coming economy, weather, climate and the political scene for years to come. Only the generation changes, not the cycle. The new economics anticipates the cycle and acts intelligently to maximize profits and minimize losses.

We still have a lot to learn about how to do it. It is somewhat analogous to following morning to evening routines, then again to bed until morning to complete the cycle. The night-side of the cycle is the analogous recession. When we have big storms, tornadoes, hurricanes that roar through the night we have the equivalent of a depression because of its length and after-effect.

Politicians promise but cannot deliver relief, unless by accident, after the fact from events of the times. Economists theorize and agree to disagree. Ministers pray for heavenly guidance since there is little else they can do. Social workers cover the problems with paperwork and throw money at social problems. Farmers look to the heavens for rain or relief from rain and to Washington for financial help. Native Indians have rain dances exhorting their rain gods to deliver water from the passing clouds to their parched crops.

Bankers ask the FRB to lower interest rates to help increase their profits and make more funds available, hoping more borrowers will appear to finance new homes, cars, plant crops, fund new industry and commercial projects.

Who raised, or who lowered interest rates anyway? Which is the cause and which event is the effect? The psychological advantage of leveraging to buy something signifies the stage of the investment cycle relative to inflation. The more intense the demand, the higher the rates as the risks continue to rise. Parallel the stock market and retail sales and you can see the credit risk developing. Somewhere, the savvy money managers and investors just quietly get off the trading game and let the novice carry the buying into the tops of the good news rallies.

People marry most often near the peak of the 18.5-year and 37- and 55.5-year cycle and divorce more near to the bottom of the 18-year cycle citing irreconcilable differences and money problems. What else would you expect? They build and buy homes at the same points in time. Their babies are conceived nearer to the peak. Fewer are born near the 18.5-year low. Strange, is it not? Many call this the generational cycle.

Prosperity is greatest just after the peak of the cycle along with bonuses, and worst after the bottom has passed. This cycle gives a right angle turn, a saw toothed wave like form in data at each extreme point—a sudden change of trend direction. This is the premise used by technicians for Point and Figure financial charting of stocks as a method of tracking the markets.

Other waveforms give undulating (numerical) curves when plotted on graph paper with the numbers swinging back and forth but with rounded tops and bottoms. Exponential rising stock markets as an example into the late 1990's, in the mid-1960's, and late 1920's increase the rate of rise for three times and usually signal a top (55-6-year) when the demand reaches almost a vertical day-to-day move as in the ninth year of the 18.5-year cycle from the previous cycle inception. That is the way it was from 1970 low to 2000 crest.

Moving averages of 50 and 200-day periods, believed to have been invented by Joe Granville, are used to cut across these price index swings. At critical, longer and terminal points they tend to cross each other near cycle turning points.

This is the ratio of 4 to 1 period. These cycles combine and form saw toothed waves of sales, profits, and head counts of employees, inventories, water consumption and energy demand. They are useful and historically test the trend of the price/index averages. Often they open new knowledge opportunities for the businessman. When sales volume crosses below the 200-day moving average line, the 50-day average, already below it and the average itself begins to turn down by becoming a (weekly) smaller number, we know the trend failure has occurred and a recessive period is beginning. The dark clouds are forming over the economy.

It is difficult to separate the cycles into individual elements and to identify the exact time, period or length. Much of our valuation of events is subjective, not objective and so we distort the facts to fit our own beliefs and circumstance. Time is the fourth dimension—length, width, depth and events over time.

The time cycle-period secret is only partially noted in this book outlined for the remainder of this first decade. The author invites you to share in this ancient re-discovery and to free yourself from living with ignorance as proposed and perpetuated by the educational system, even through college and post graduate days. This is one area needing a lot of research. For the ten-year old student to learn how to sort the elements to fulfill his best in his future life he should not be contaminated with false claims. How can we re-educate a Ph. D Economist, or a BA? Change the system! The educational system is fully indoctrinated.

Perhaps one of the greatest historical studies of the past millennium was when empires and nations reached their final eminence and then began to decline as noted in Chapter 1.

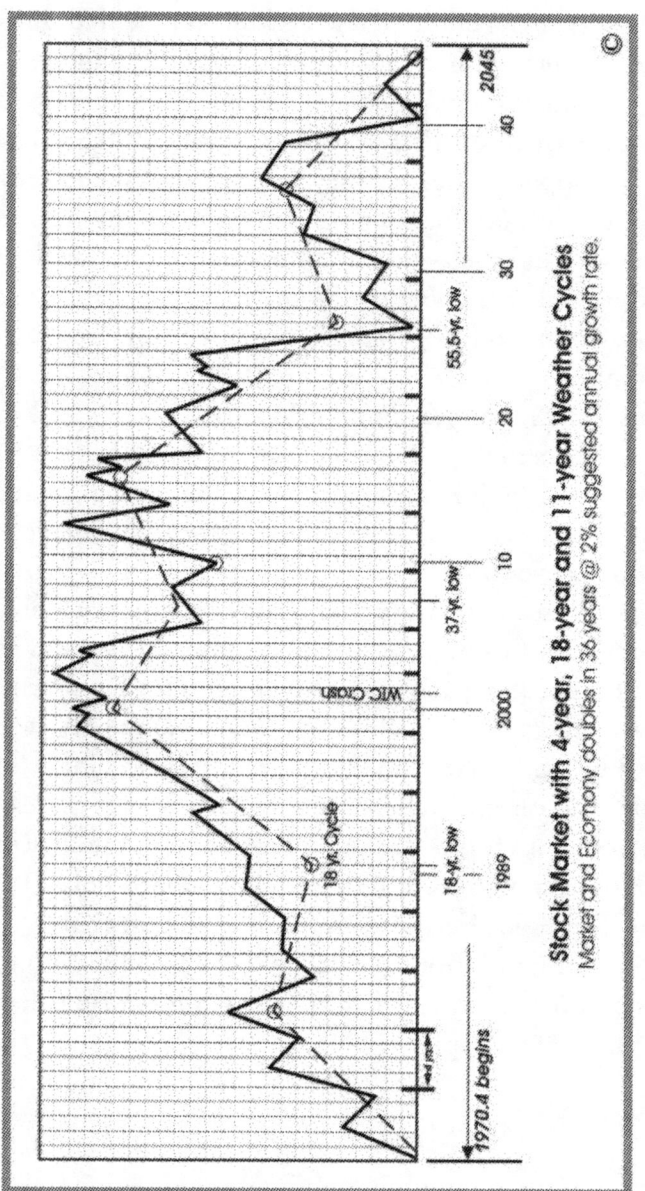

Chart 2

With the **Crash** concept we can project major economic and market lows as well as document market highs. Market cycles ride upon the rate of change of underlying cyclical events thus giving us undulating statistical data. Because these cycles continue to repeat and have been verified back into the 16th and 17th centuries, there is little risk to acting more aggressively in the markets. Government regulatory bodies should realign their management policies to modify the extremes of the cycles. Tax averaging over four years would reduce the pain of recessions. We can stabilize world economies just knowing when the fever pitch is to be the greatest and when discouraging events are at their worst.

Chart 2—Stock Market with 4-year, 18-year and 11-year
Weather Cycles

This is revolutionary to the masses and probably unbelievable to the businessman and many politicians. The cycle effect has been formulated. Where do we stand today in this spiral of civilization? Are we doomed by forces beyond our ken to understand? That is the way life experience actualizes. Events beyond our control do control our fate to a greater extent than most believe. Noting these turning points gives us a chance to prosper and protect ourselves from many forms of disasters instead of following the crowds.

We fill our lives theorizing causes and effects as it strikes our affairs not knowing why or when changes will appear. Some hope for the change, others like the way things are going. We enjoy the petty, the subjective, give an emotional response to relate to another and continue to search for reasons for living. It is more than "the children" that drive us to pursue our inborn genetic coded agendas and to achieve against great odds, just to survive.

It is the knowing insight that there is something better than what we have today in our prosperity and creative endeavors, that causes us to try to ride the fastest mount, overcome the powers that limit, search for a new constellation, gain access to the energy currents that drive our lives up the river of change to greater moments of glory than ever dreamed of.

Why would any man want to ride a rocket into space for an average pay of $65,000 a year with the possibility that the rocket might explode under him or he become lost in space in the solar system? There is something a man must feel exists beyond that which he senses, but he cannot see. He sets his values and sights to find this energy of life living on the vicarious edge as a way to challenge his being. This may be western man's Jihad to martyrdom giving a purpose to life other than procreation and servitude to a religion, job or sense of empire under a tyrant.

Some of us become great scientists, engineers, doctors, teachers, military strategists; others become rich without reason, many just survive, some become great family men and women and leaders in improving society. A few still search for the Holy Grail, others the secrets of life in genetic codes, movements under a microscope, in a laboratory. Most exist as part of the generic composition of labor, servitude so to speak, in a regular career job.

Others among us are evil from birth till death regardless of social stature, title or wealth accumulated in life. Are they not the counterparts for those who are creative, successful and objective? Sometimes we see the truth mirrored in the lives of other people, but refuse to accept it as being part of our own selves, just as though we really exist in reverse to the mirror, different only in our minds eye. Is this not the devil in man and woman versus the Christian/Moslem God, the heavenly beings, or the creative goodness of beings? There is always the counter part of society, situation or belief, the ying-yang of the Chinese culture. The bogey-man is always with us.

In life, man performs his role as he was created to do, as also woman does just like the cycle within her when it excites its positive or negative values assigned in the curve over time in the fourth dimension, the estrus cycle. Animals remain animals to do what they are designed to do during their lives. Birds love to fly and do what birds must do to survive. So does man follow the natural laws found within his own genetic code? What would you do with your working hours if you did not have to theorize about the turn of the cycle for your product or investments? You could have a much greater leisure life, make more money, and go to the office only to serve a special problem or need.

5

Can We Trust the Cycles?

Can we trust these cycles to repeat?

Absolutely! They are not man-made, but have existed in nature for as many years as man has been able to measure and count. The risk is in not having knowledge of cause and a means of tracking cycle turning points; it is in ignoring them in the equation of time. Not enough knowledge is like needing another gallon of gas to get over the hill and home.

They are real, having operated for thousands of years. Only a few researchers have succeeded in isolating the primary trend cycles. It is a complicated job, but once the research correlates and projections hit the turns within a range of a few days, then investor and businessman alike should not fear them.

Knowing when they change and when the public mood begins anew and investments again appear as being desirable, lowers the financial risk. They offer opportunities for the student of change to get in on the ground floor of a new business trend and to maximize the opportunity.

Thus it has been stated as the old saying "Buy Low, Sell High!" Also, buy on the rumor of new management, products, and ideas and sell when the news is reported.

This latter point applies mostly to short-term trades up to one year. Some investments lead such as retail sales, while the rally of the transportation indices and trucking/airline stocks signal the final stage of the market and economic rallies. Shipping and travel during plush earn-

39

ings times are usually at the end of a bountiful market season. These are usually the points when mergers are being made. Numerous mergers and IPO's (Initial Public Offerings) are signals of topping action. There aren't many taking place when things are slow and uncertain, but that is when the natural merging should begin to maximize profits and to minimize costs. Business does it the other way, often when the competition is peaking and they don't need any more competition, so they merge to reduce the cost of operations.

6

Coming Energy Crisis

The Coming Energy Crisis is Here, Now!

It started in California in the year 2000. It was a hot spring, dry and burgeoning with illegal immigrants crossing the borders looking for seasonal work and migrating in greater numbers than ever before. They were heading for the big cities and a few to the farmlands and vineyards. It was destined to be one of the hottest summers in many generations. It was also destined to be the end of the era of Global Warming ideas.

It was a time when electricity had been deregulated after 1996 in California. It was at the peak of the housing construction 18-year cycle and it was the season of the 11.1-year sunspot cycle, which always produces high winds and Santa Ana firestorm conditions throughout the west.

The four-year cycle had made its top in the early spring of the year 1998. The next peak is in 2002. Wow! How can anyone be so precise and confident? No problem! This is the way life is, a routine generation-to-generation, cycle-to-cycle. We cannot forever be crossing the great void without end or in a mindless direction. Man would finally die in the struggle never having found anything familiar or helpful. The order of the solar system has remained constant, only man cannot remember, having such a short life span and being part of the problem of solar life forms.

Power bills suddenly ballooned to triple and some to sextuple, above ordinary summer levels as air conditioners came on to cool the offices and malls. It is contended by Loretta Sanchez on April 13, 2002 that Enron manipulated demand by futures trading and facility shut downs for maintenance. Forest fires abounded and the hot winds blew off-shore as Santa Ana winds and then four days later they blew eastward over the mountain passes to the eastern prairies as Chinooks. The winds have always blown this way and always will no matter how the ecologists proclaim their dominance and desires.

Everything was burning along with our national forests from border to border in the west. Without air-conditioning and cooling systems, it was still unbearable inside factories, shops and homes. Big city residential buildings were furnaces of accumulated daytime heat for several days with elder citizens cooped up in non-air conditioned units. They died in bed while fanning themselves.

A rate price cap for electricity was held in place in California, but wholesale prices were free to float, as Loretta Lynch, Chairman of the California Public Utilities Commission decided, forcing utilities to buy in the spot market only. That was the law she and the legislature had devised and it had been signed by then Governor Pete Wilson. Does not make much sense does it? But politicians make strange bedfellows at times. We need a total and scientific revision to economic and market theory as well as rules based on sound principles, not political hay. Cycles control, not man.

7

Population is in Free Fall

Declining birth rates dominate western culture.

At the same time, women are having fewer children, and then don't rear them, but do use subsidized nurseries. Whose culture is being delivered to the newborn Americans? The babysitters? Minorities? Cultural religions? Have babies become the pawns of our future? Why do we not want children in western cultures?

A sudden increase in death rates of seniors and a return of Hispanics to Mexico while the United States is in recession over the next decade of years could turn our nation into a shrinking economy.

Still, many academics publish in Science Magazine. Their projection is for a doubling population into the fourth millennium. The prophecy implied with ending global warming in 2000, suggests this shrink packaging of America is pending and we will find fewer jobs available, fewer schools, smaller cities, etc.

Liberals are not gleeful because consumption will decline and suddenly opportunities to take over for a socialist society may disappear. If the public is not dependant on them, how can they control from Washington? Or, perhaps the in UN, The Hague, Netherlands, World Court and Europe's new headquarters.

Fertility rates are a major problem in Russian lands also. The population is getting sicker every year, the birth rate is falling as disintegrating healthcare, environment hazards and poor nutrition prevail. Fertility rate is down to 1.3 per female. Half of Russian men die, before they can retire, at age 60 from heart disease, alcoholism and smoking. Ten to 25% of Russian couples are infertile. Infant mortality is on the rise with 10% dying (under five) of infection. Within 20 years it is projected that Russia will have a population under 100 million, smaller than Japan's 125 million from the 145 million current counts. Some suggest 95 or fewer million of the northern Slavic nation will survive. Will Japan begin to shrink, too?

This is not only a Russian problem but is appearing throughout Europe, and is likely a world disaster gaining speed. Africa is projected to remain a disaster with shorter life spans and higher death rates from female abortions and rampant HIV disease. There seems to be a topping out of favorable human growth conditions throughout the world. Islam nations continue to breed in their poverty living and with the Koran's admonishments.

In Discover Magazine, September 4, 2001, p 23, it is noted that of the sexually transmitted diseases, the following ranked worst to least are: Human Papillomavirus 5.5 million, Trichomoniasis 5 million, Chlamydia 3. million, Herpes 1 million, Gonorrhea 650 thousand, Hepatitis B 120 thousand, Syphilis 70 thousand and HIV 40 thousand new cases annually. In Africa HIV is 50% of the problem.

We have yielded to a group of sexual deviants who are closely infected with the HIV virus to attack the smallest of our social disease problems. In Africa, it is the major problem. This shows the power of vocal media groups. We have had to emphasize this social condition over all other medical problems. Now that anthrax and small pox has become a social issue, the loss of funding seems inevitable as our talent pool seeks cures for other mass destruction illnesses. We may spend much too much of our resources on a single or a potential disease and fail to discern the surprise that nature may impose on us. It will be an expensive period into the 2008-10 lows.

8

Federal Reserve Board Seems Helpless

It is interesting to note how the FRB cut interest rates 2% in the first four months of year 2001, and still the stock markets have failed to return to Bull Market status. Brokers and money managers are complaining trying to hang the problems onto Alan Greenspan and then George W. Bush, 43rd President. In May, the FRB dropped another .25 basis points off the Discount Rate (inter-bank overnight lending rate). A rally followed on Wednesday Thursday and Friday May 18th 2001 pressing the 30% rally resistance level. Could it be crossed? If it could hold two days over the old downtrend line of tops, it will probably challenge the previous major high. That is, the Dow Jones Industrial Average (DJIA) checking out the old highs.

After nearly two weeks trying to hold over 11,100 the DJIA fell under the magic number on May 29. The broader S&P500, Russell 2000 and NASDAQ Comp remain substantially below their old high about 48% lower for the NASDAQ Index, 15% for the S&P500. The markets turned lower in spite of the broker and analyst talk of great buying opportunities. The only problem is they have a false god in FRB interest rate manipulation called monetarism.

This is the control system that J. M. Keynes devised in order to create the good economic times. Has it too failed us? Are we looking for a new theory that we can depend upon? Have we ever had a good indicator that never failed, or at least was good for 90% of the time? If you know of one, bring it out now. We need it. Into December 2001 the Fed lowered the Discount Rate for the eleventh time to 1.75%, from 6% (5-16-00) a depression low. The recovery is not occurring. It is weak, many stocks still crashing.

Does that not shake your confidence that the market and the economic response were not more impressive? What has gone wrong? How will the huge trillion dollar revenue surplus contribute to the recovery? (It's gone.) Can it? With the war in Afghanistan and elections in 2002, the money has is already consumed the surplus, along with pork.

How much of the surplus will ever be returned to the taxpayer? Small increments may occur. Somehow, it looks like the bureaucracy and politicians will grab the money for make-work pork projects as in the Great Depression with the PWA, the PAW, the WAP, WPA, the alphabet agencies, APW, the AWP alphabet agencies, which were once created in the Great Depression to save the nation. They only saved the bureaucrats who were living high and on expense accounts too.

Based on the Budget passed in May 2001, the maximum refund for a married couple was $600. It was mailed to taxpayers based upon the last 0-9 digits of the Social Security number. Nothing is to be available to higher income taxpayers or lower under $25M non-taxpayers. Over ten years, it looks like darn little of the taxes will be returned to taxpayers, or even to low-income non-taxpayers. The political battle continues among socialists and capitalists with overtones of communism and the Islamic Jihad.

Considering the normal 4% average rate of inflation per year, we are not even treading water. It looks like the same old game is being played by the elected officials on the public. "We'll spend it on pork projects that Congress chooses. We have to keep the cash so we can help you 'all." That's only the author's opinion. Prove him wrong! The sunset clause is at ten years—2011. The law is then dead. We've got a war to win! Politicians need the funds to buy votes in coming elections.

Andrews is reporting another eight years of crashing investments. Are you watching your capital and retirement money? Are you going to join the soup kitchen crowd in 2008-10?

The rule still applies "Never fight the Feds when it tightens or loosens the money supply." Is it possible this rule is now wrong? Has the FRB failed us? Is it time to change the game, and get a new theory of economics to work better than Keynesian Economics? Cycles are the only natural controlling event in the history of man and are followed religiously, or naturally, over eons of time. It is time we got to work on a real understanding of the economics of nature and how they control us so we can work with them. We have been fighting political economic ideas since before 1776 when Jefferson began to develop the financial rules of the Republic. Until then, it was the king or potentate that made the rules.

It seems that few of the appointed and elected politicians have any training in cause and effect economics. Even to have had Economics 101 would help. With our Keynesian thinking as the dominant economic game plan of the FRB, pump priming and manipulating money supply is supposed to limit recessions and maximize the good times. Economic ignorance still prevails in the legislatures and halls of modern government. A test of their skills is on now to prove they can control the economy or else they have taken a side road to Confusion City that mythical destination of eternal prosperity, plenty and without struggle. Nirvana seems to be the goal of all mankind down through history. No one has ever found it except in the mind, the expectation of a life that is acceptable.

In looking over the statistics of the past 100 market years, there is no evidence that the FRB and its governors have achieved any stabilization other than to chase out the small local banks, who previously printed their own money for years. That was when gold was the base for currency. We have no base now, just promises that Uncle Sam will pay off. Finally the Discount Rate close the year at 1.25%, a Great Depression year low. By limiting who could print currency it helped a great deal on a local basis but mostly in commerce over long distances. Scoundrels are still found everywhere forging documents and currencies. Bad money still drives out good money so we honor counterfeit currencies and burn it promptly. There are many clever printers out there in alien and domestic lands.

Long ago it was found this Keynesian pump priming management had limited applications and worked coincidently, not the result of skillful money management. Thus, the huge government Treasury debt from pump priming beginning in the 30's until we are money junkies today which brought us to the huge national debt of year 2000.

Suddenly the taxation from a burgeoning stock market taking profits after accumulated low cost positions from the 37-year lows of the early seventies and possibly from the thirties among family heirs, created a huge surplus and the pay down became possible.

It is no wonder all the economists and market makers are complaining that Greenspan is still keeping money too tight because the market did not respond from his Fed Funds rate decreases. Long-term rates are controlled by market demand and supply. Another decrease at the Open Market meeting in May 2001 of ¼% reduction in Discount Rate was made. Nothing happened in the markets or the economy. In December 2001 the Discount Rate to the bankers finally reached 1.75% as low as in the Great Depression years. No results appeared that were not showing before the final drop in year 2001, except a brief rally in the stock market testing the 10,000 level where the 200-day moving average line was beginning to level off. Greenspan was feeling, reaching out for his short hair strands to pull on his scalp. Frustration? You bet! He was at wits end. What if all his effort had been in vain? The system is broke and now he realizes he is helpless!

Finally the Discount Rate closed the year at 1.25%. What if that reduction does not turn our economy "on?" Should we begin to study Japan's failure to recover, also as a case study, even with Japan's interest rates below 1% today?

Stimulating industry by reducing money costs, like conserving fuel, does not alter the trend dominated by cyclical forces. We seem to have a production overcapacity problem too in this country as well as in imports in many industries. This is still consuming capital and must shrink to reach equilibrium before interest rates can stabilize.

M2 and M3 in the U.S. (Money Supply in circulation) have continued their steady rises for about a year since summer 2000 and still the market and economy are stumbling. Greenspan had raised interest rates and tightened money supplies to keep the economy from overheating into the summer. The economy continued to roll in spite of the squeeze. Is there something we do not know, officially, about what causes markets to rise then fall in prices and then employment levels to rise and fall, and interest rates to rise and fall regularly, in spite of FRB actions? This is a forbidden area of research since no one has proposed a new theory of economic interest. All these economists, being the confused opinion of the times, were trained in Keynesian Theory as the great manipulator of societies. Even Russia finally accepted the theory devised by an Englishman after the Berlin Wall was taken down and the USSR broke into nationalist pieces.

Until the old theory completely crashes, accepting a new concept of what causes prices to rise and fall among other similar events, is unlikely to be accepted, even with the evidence overwhelmingly presented in the papers and with the new regulatory ideas stated here. Will 2010 give us a new theory?

Spot markets are the highest priced source for any commodity and without long-term contractual pricing advantages. This is the market of desperation when management failures of an organization strike reality because of a shortfall in planned supply. Traders drool at such prospects. These energy traders squeezed the last nickel out of paranoid energy demand until the system broke. Enron, one of the largest fuel managers and energy providers, declared bankruptcy. The fallout will take many honest companies with the write-offs, just as in the 1929 period; the banks were reduced to rubble and managers became educated office and retail store operators to survive. The author remembers many of them.

9

Chinese Threat Remains

The Chinese vow to bring war, an attack to our coastal cities within the next ten years. Some experts see a move in just two years. They are serious since they have already secured both ends of the Panama Canal, a base near Bermuda, Long Beach Naval Shipyard and various other cargo transfer points within the Mojave desert and central valley, closed military bases and within major market shipping points of nearby states as well as in other nations of the western hemisphere. There are reports of rearming Cuba, also sending in Chinese trained fifth columnists to work on Chinese projects in many of the countries of South America. We may have new reports out of Africa covering similar Chinese intentions. Will the Chinese succeed where Hitler failed? And now they want the Olympics in 2008!

Japan, you are being reminded, began its economic power move by developing opportunities in exclusive leather and other commodity purchase agreements (much as Hitler did with blocked currency exchanges in the 30's) exchanging agricultural equipment to developing nations, buying expensive land in major cities and developments by using government subsidy with very low interest rates.

Subsidies were common in order to break into another nation's market, and they then disallowed the target nation to exchange products to cover the cost of imports requiring Yen currency. Thus, they controlled the other nation without an invasion. This same tactic is being applied by the Chinese, as did the Nazis. It is being used to infiltrate many western hemisphere countries. Even Russia had tried it before and it was only the start of WW II that ended the blocked currency practices.

Japan ran into reality in 1989 as the 18-year Real Estate cycle struck. The lending practice of "anything was ok when used as collateral for land, stock markets, corporate exports, investors, etc. purchases" has turned out to be a terrible price. Margin borrowing was heavily used. The collapse of banks from the decline in raw land values, ranching for beef and golf courses and Real Estate values ended the caper.

In the fall of 2001, Japan Inc. was still on its back. In April 2001, a new Prime Minister Junichiro Koizumi promised to right their economy. First he began to slash wasteful public-sector spending, improve trash disposal, urban development and anti-pollution works by spending part of the proceeds from the 48-year old auto and fuel tax law. We will observe since Koizumi come in near the top of the current 18-year cycle.

The second 18-year cycle is now striking the Japanese economy again, and they still have not recovered from the last blow like the U.S. markets and economies had done in the 90's. The U.S. of A. had the internet high tech boost to its economy and a reduction of military spending needs due to the recent Russian Revolution and break-up.

Will this same cycle shake up the Chinese economy like it did in Tokyo and in the European Union similarly? Will this regional problem cause Beijing to lose control of its socialist/communist government? We will observe as other economies of the world too begin to implode and sober up their leaders. A tax on Internet transactions by the U.S. could easily trigger many hi-tech collapses, including Microsoft. Telecommunication companies would likely be rescued from declining phone revenues.

10

A Debilitating Monopoly: OPEC

OPEC (Organization of Petroleum Exporting Countries) is a near monopoly. It acts "as one" trying to hold the price and supply of oil at a favorable extreme price level compared to the cost of other alternative fuels. Its pricing practice acts as a tax on every user of petroleum products around the world. We know that industry pays no taxes since these are just costs to be passed onto the consumer in higher prices just as are corporate income taxes.

A move among legislators just recently gave hope that Congress might reduce corporate taxes. Perhaps Congress will introduce a 17% consumer tax on sales of merchandise, on everything. It would have to drop the mindless growth of tax lists on everything else if it is to succeed. The great risk is that the public is fearful that once the 17% is established, it can be raised easily and often. That would create an angry population of taxpayers. Why 17% on retail consumer purchases? Income furnishes a cycle of about three to four times before it is consumed: 3 x 17 = 51% or more, currently paid in taxes by wage earners, an increase!

One of the risks is that Congress still has the idea that the public is capable of absorbing unlimited taxes. History has proven there are limits and we see it in Argentina as the nation goes bankrupt. It can happen here.

Still the public thinks corporations should pay more and continues the myth as to who pays the taxes. Has the Congress ever studied (cause and effect), basic economics?

Universities and colleges have reached the state of affairs to believe and teach that money belongs to government. It alone allows the worker and corporation the privilege to exist by following their rules. It alone allows a modicum of profits to be double-taxed when paid to stockholders.

If the nation has no alternative fuel then an oil price increase by OPEC is just an increased tax from a non-government agency because it raises the costs for all levels of society. It is essentially another excise tax, a devaluation of the purchasing power of the currency, leaving less income for food, housing, clothing and enjoyment of life. It reduces natural prosperity.

Assets flow out of the country through the banking system and into the monopolistic nations' bank accounts. This is barely reported. It is the modern form of piracy and a squeeze play on nations with little oil product.

When OPEC took away the oil supply in year 2000 (like in 1973 also) and also raised wellhead prices, the U.S. public found electrical and heating bills tripled, at the least, adding another load to the annual tax burden. This put the domestic tax level now over 42% to 49.2% ranging up to a 57% rate.

In addition, all food and manufactured goods prices were raised to cover the increased cost of production and distribution.

This energy tax has pushed the total tax burden to probably over 60% of average incomes. Commuters pay more, autos cost more, clothes and rents are more expensive and food is up some 15% over 2000 levels. This level of tax is absolutely intolerable!

Labor Department's COLI (Cost of Living Index) has been edited in recent decades to exclude many of the elements that reduce disposable incomes to taxpayers, suggesting little or no inflation remains. When the majority of people involved in a field of expertise agree on price and/or production levels, perhaps even of politics, the upset is due.

In Spring 2001, Venezuelan, Mexican and Colombian representatives met in Caracas, revived a six-year old trade bloc called the Group of Three to "help stabilize" oil prices.

Hugo Chavez of Venezuela was also head of the OPEC organization. He was a socialist/communist leader of his country. We should not expect any favors from him and his associates to relieve the oil shortfall for the North American consumer outside their own countries. Socialists believe they can set the prices and demand a given profit for the state in lieu of taxes. Here is again evidence of support for the Islamic belief that they alone should rule the world. It is the belief that socialism will inherit the earth.

Perhaps the majority of the people in Europe, Asia, China, India, South America, Mexico and those smaller nations sitting on an oil pool agree that reaching the magic number of around 2/3rds of the populations is now here. Will the upset suddenly strike? If these believers can raise prices and restrict production of energy during a severe depression, which is likely to appear in the next six years, then our Capitalism and freedom has been surrendered.

There is another element to this equation. Our energy technology has developed new propulsion systems that require little or no oil products. These technologies are expected to begin to be used within these next ten years in the military primarily. Then, as experience and understanding produce efficiencies that allow the applications to be included in aircraft, auto and power generation centers the phase out of oil use could place the entire oil industry of the world in jeopardy. Arab power would grind down to infighting among their neighbors as to who gets the oil to sell this year.

Environmentalists protest any time domestic oil producers want to drill, build a pipeline, refinery, hi-line, install a generator or even refine oil differently from erratic formulas written by environmentalists who demand it for certain local counties, etc. Will this new energy system destroy the ecological programs we deal with at every turn?

Obstructionist environmentalists are like parasites living on the productivity of this once great nation much as leaches, those blood sucking parasites and parasite growths which attach themselves to the organs or bloodstream like worms, which then eat us from within the structure of our lives and our own creativity.

Our vitality is soon gone and we, as the nation, develop a coma while the university Ph.D. doctors struggle with a thousand theories of the cause of this malaise. They too, being part of the problem, do not recognize anything other than money supplies and power (noted by the FRB as M2, M3, M4) as valid economics and only complicate the struggle for the patient's recovery by asking for more budget increase (taxes).

Keynes is dead and he only had a theory, which was adopted, without testing, into perpetuity. Most other nations have accepted the practices of the Fed. Now that it is failing us, what might we fall back on? There is nothing pending in the textbooks.

In winter of 2000-1, natural gas and gasoline prices at the pump were jumped about 1/3rd by marketers. They were priced at the pump being greatest in the major cities and remote regions, as valued by unleaded prices. The regular quality was priced around $2.00 per gallon and higher at freeway off ramps. A range of up to 20 cents more for premium qualities required by some vehicles brought the price paid to $2.30. It stabilized at this level for nearly five months. It then began to decline abruptly as talk of new drilling was reported, opening of the Alaskan reserves, new discoveries, etc.

With talk of running the price to near $3.00 from near $1.50 the year earlier in spring, it was a threat. By Mother's Day 2001 the price was near $2.40 in major cities for premium and $1.99 for unleaded. That's more than doubling the retail price, taxes remaining constant, and more than doubling oil's marketing profits. Sales taxes on gasoline brought in additional tax revenue.

Transporters and processors using natural gas, oil and gasoline as feedstock quietly raised prices on all products. All those oil mergers in the past ten years have eliminated the small independent marketers by price manipulation.

Now, there are only a few major oil companies remaining. The handful of remaining, major oil marketing companies don't need to sit down and collude to run the prices up. They are price gouging in every way they can and, so far, in the past decade Justice Department has kept approving their mergers. They now have vertical integration and control all levels of the industry from drilling to pumping.

We have lost control of the Justice System, courts, police and the administration of the laws. The Sherman Anti-Trust Act is considered an anachronism to world economic schemes.

Will President Bush seek to control these arrogant pricing practices? Will the public hold them in contempt and approve penalties for their unreasonable price gouging? They being "oil-men" in real life, the President and Vice-President are easily targets of mistrust and divisive political practices by the media. Their action belies this concept in actual political practice. On April 11, 2002 a military coup removed Chavez from office.

There was little mention of this in the newspapers. The press must have a conflict of interest between advertisers and the need for the public to know.

The press was given fourth estate rights because they were supposed to report these egregious acts of monopoly and abuse of economic and political power to the people. Should the press be indicted and the fourth amendment be taken away from them, or be modified?

Any shopper realizes that a 20-dollar bill hardly goes for a bag of groceries today and only buys 1/3rd the gallons of fuel it did a few years ago. They do not report on anything that informs the public except to patronize their advertisers and their own privilege of publishing.

Why did we fight the Gulf War, anyway? Certainly not to deliver these monopolistic practices to OPEC and now, not again to the internationalized oil marketing/producer groups, not the oil interests with headquarters outside of the USA, or to the "friends of Bush" the 41st President. How did this happen in just a decade? Who got the pay-off, if not, who turned his attention away from protecting the United States interests? Answer: Who was the 42nd President?

It is the American taxpayer who funded the war and paid the price! Why should private corporations get the profits?

Should we drill in Alaska, who would control the oil produced from our Arctic reserves? At present, it would become one of the major producers and marketers of domestic oil. So why should we deliver more monopoly oil to them when they have no obligation to lower prices for a fair profit for their services. Should the American consumer share in this bonanza in some way? While Arco was managing the Alaskan pipe-line and production, the oil during high priced months, was being shipped to Japan. Should we allow this to recur if we develop new Alaskan resources?

It is interesting to note that when the major partner in the Alaskan oil venture Arco was merged with the Mobil Oil organization, it was only a few weeks after the approval by the Justice Department that the California oil prices were raised exorbitantly and promptly.

Certainly, we need to redress this issue since it is inevitable that it will become part of the cause of the Crash of 2008.

There seems to be no one responsible in government anymore nor are we capable of invoking anti-trust laws because of many oil mergers. They have made themselves into international companies and have slipped headquarters into overseas countries to avoid such monopoly charges. Our commercial tanker fleet is registered in foreign countries to avoid labor standards, taxes and responsibility for losses.

Perhaps we should revise and revitalize the Sherman Act to include OPEC producers, since they do maintain huge bank balance accounts in this country, merchandise their products as fuel for motorcars, raw materials for the chemical industries, and they are as guilty as the remnants of our oil industries of price fixing and manipulation. Of course, oil prices are excessive in all countries since oil is priced in dollars. Surely, the other nations using oil products are willing to join with us to act against this usurious monopoly!

11

Inflation! Inflation?

The inflation creep, where is it? It is there and doing well! Groceries, drug store prices, gasoline, auto services, lumber, land, taxes all continue to creep up. Have you read the nickel and penny taxes and fees posted to your phone bill this past year? On Friday May 11, 2001, Gold gapped over its resistance line and began an uptrend. Inflation is on its way. It may pause at times as when the WTC towers were destroyed, but it will return when the dollar begins to weaken against the main currencies.

First of every year the drug and pharmaceutical companies raise prices, change package sizes and contents. Insurance companies raise the co-pay amount. So do the retail merchants begin to fill coffee cans with 11.5 oz contents instead of 16 oz old sized cans. Result is smaller package sizes at same price, and so it goes.

By slowly raising the temperature of the water for the lobster in the pot until it is too late for him to jump out and run for the sea, his innards are cooked and served to the restaurant's customers.

Agricultural products are still under pressure, but when priced at retail, there is an increasing spread for the middlemen—producer to retailer. Higher energy prices increase delivery costs with surcharges as well as processing costs, then labor costs, etc. Inflation continues and is felt by the fixed income people as well as the poorer laborer.

Bread in the 2000-1 period rose 20%, but when combined with meats and cheeses, the increase was buried in the summaries. Much of the increase is due to added hidden taxes on the manufacturer and middlemen while the consumer complains. Some consumers cannot see the change because of the pricing razzle-dazzle every week and club cards. Sales prices are not really sales, nor equal to discount prices. Discounts are not really discounts or savings but the razzle-dazzle of merchandisers.

Those "$ savings" by shopping at grocery stores are so phony that it is embarrassing to many checkers. Without discount cards (similar to Blue Chip and Green Stamps) for the regular customers, the cost of groceries would be reported to be way over government index statistics. Even automobiles can be bought much cheaper than posted prices. Computer internet users can compare prices among dealers and even buy from -autobytel.com- (auto by telephone) at well below the posted prices.

Paper goods, while in surplus supply in early 2001, were finding retail prices up 20%, except at sales times when they were slightly higher than regular prices of the previous year. As gluts at the mills are reported for paper products, there seemed to be no price reductions at retail. We may have to wait until the economy reaches bottom after 2004 and 2008 for real savings.

Holding price structures with the profit structure intact is admirable, but it is more likely that there is a semi-monopoly in the local area or industry. Eventually competition will move in and force prices lower into line, when the game is exposed. It does take time for the market to adjust, unless our Justice Department begins to take action to reduce the merging and collusive price action.

12

Collusion

Oil monopolies are nothing new and everyone in business likes to get greedy as user dependency opportunities develop or are created.

In the late 19th century with the railroads and against the producers of oil and refinery products, Rockefeller built an empire. It was so vicious that it led to its break-up, the great oil monopoly, by the Justice Department.

He had kickbacks from the transport industry, the railroad carriers against the other oil refinery and marketing companies, since the automobile had become more popular than the horse.

Highways and airlines did not exist and rails were the latest fad but an almost unregulated means of transporting oil. He used them to build his empire. Most of his techniques are now illegal because of the Sherman Anti-Trust Act provisions. He raised the price of oil when it was real cheap, like ten cents a barrel by adding his 25¢ per barrel rail kickback fee (actually $2.50 per barrel) from the railroads from other oil shippers. It has been a while since reviewing these figures, but they are substantially correct. The same game is being played today.

Now it's OPEC doing a similar thing to world users. How we will break this control of OPEC remains to be seen, but it will be broken one day only when the U.S. of A is less dependant on oil and others are finding alternate energy sources like nuclear, solar, etc.

There are several ways it can happen. One is a charge by Justice Department of collusion, or monopolistic mergers in the U.S. of A, or sudden drop in oil demand due to layoffs, recession in the U.S. of A while producers must pump and store oil while building inventories world-wide. A combination of events appears most likely by autumn '01. Someday new energy concepts will be found and tried and our propulsion systems will change leaving oil and coal behind. Next price low for oil @ $10.00 per barrel is 2008.

13

Inflation Will Now Follow

Watch the price of gold to confirm the onset, which it did on May 11, 2001. Gold is already on the move higher! That is another opportunity for investors. Lumber has doubled in the past few months and real estate prices (stored labor and materials) will parallel increases like in the '70's. Such thinking must be verified by the actual commodity demand. In October 2001, gold began to sell off, lumber prices faltered as new starts disappeared. That was a one-month slowdown it seems.

So, why should housing increase and deflation remain in the commodity market? First point seems to be that housing is a refuge from the stock market for people who sold at higher prices than found today. They await a signal to reenter the markets. Upgrading began and moving into retirement homes, not trailers and flats for these people, but acreage home sites away from the big city problems. Gated communities and gentlemen farmers position themselves away from the crime and local politics of suburbia. In California, grapes are overplanted, but that is always the way it is at cycle tops.

Second, if commodities are still falling then manufacturing is on the decline, because we over-stimulated and overbuilt our industrial capacity. In addition, we have simplified many manufacturing operations by assembling overseas parts brought into the plants to be made into products. Here again we over-anticipated our needs and built more inventory than consumers could utilize. Applications for computer controls and simplification programs for commerce and industry reduced the need for many personnel. Jobs were eliminated. Unemployment claims were consumed.

In other words, demand fell off. We pulled in our horns in fall 2000. Now we have to work off the excesses. Remember how hard we were running right into the last few days of the millennium? We stockpiled for the false crash from computer numbers not tracking over 1999.99. It didn't happen. What to do now with all the unconsumed preparations? Consume them daily.

14

Inflation Under President Johnson

It was popular to blame President Nixon, the FRB and the local taxing authorities, who mercilessly raised property taxes and increased income taxes, all the while implementing hidden taxes on everything we were using like telephones, property, auto licenses, driver license, tire excise and all sorts of highway and sales taxes. These taxes are still in place, even though they are talking of some changes, and that is where the problem rests. On rare occasions has a tax been removed.

Congress refuses to remove any tax (no party affiliations are exempt) including the telephone tax from the Spanish American war. It was finally removed in 2001 as a token to political stupidity. They do not want to set any precedent to reduce hidden and income taxes. They like to spend your money for pork projects, paying back the campaign donors with fat margins for their sometimes shabby workmanship. They feel their power when they can say "NO."

Government borrowed heavily to implement President Johnson's Great Society ideas. This added to the (COLA) cost of living. Retirement benefits expanded while the value of land rose equally and existing housing and building values climbed 11 times. Even postage stamps rose from 3-cent postcards to 20 cents. Today, it is 34 cents for a bill or letter over the minimum from 3 cents before the sixties.

The dollar was deflating and under President Nixon the gold conversion window for the dollar was closed ending the problem since foreign nations were demanding gold in exchange for acquired trade dollars. This brought us into the 18-year cycle lows of 1970 and four-year low in 1974. Real Estate foreclosures, droughts and low market prices prevailed as banks collapsed and were closed. This is a very similar economic and social period, which is being projected here for 2008-10, then again in a milder form in 2026-7.

Note the current pattern with China gaining large export balances of near $100 billion a year and then using it for price wars against us, and possibly a military war, to threaten our economic stability far more than the loss of labor's jobs.

While high employment levels occurred in year 2000 causing some labor cost rises, the number of manufacturers building overseas plants was still rising.

Now that these foreign plants produce with cheaper foreign labor, and the market is slipping for their products in our country, too, will our unemployed labor pool rise dramatically? It was 4% in autumn 2001. Will it force high unemployment costs on our industry and our government agencies? Will today's "budget surplus" be consumed by the unemployed draw down before 2010? First, we must win the terrorist war; else all this talk does not matter. We are already into the government bond market selling to get cash again.

Spring 2001 saw unemployment levels rise to the 1991 levels at the low of the economy in which William J. Clinton claimed it to be "the worst economy in history." He rode the recovery just coming in on his first election year. This was the low end of the 18-year cycle. A can't lose opportunity! Will the Democrats take over again at the 2008-10 cycle low? Here's an opportunity for a political change? Yet, we have not yet made the 18-year lows of this major cycle and deflation continues to force raw materials down. We must expect a more severe condition than seen today. If this is the bubble deflating from the early eighties, then there is much more of economic devaluation still in the works.

Will we be able to create new industries fast enough to absorb these labor components of new products being created today? Will many of these people have saved enough to retire gracefully, without full dependence on welfare and Social Security? Will this added load to the SS system then cause a collapse in the retirement benefits, currently projected for fund depletion by 2038?

Will our tax surplus remain large enough to absorb these almost indigent and growing in number retirees who depend on their market invested savings to supplement their meager savings?

Will it be wise to allow individuals the privilege of investing in the stock market equities, or bonds on their own as part of their retirement plan? After the way the markets have acted since 1999?

To look at it another way, perhaps the domestic rising unemployment problem is moot. With declining birth rates (fertility rate is around 1.8 and falling) the only thing holding the growth of the country in uptrend are a longer-lived senior element and lots of illegal aliens from around the world moving over the borders. We are developing a culture of centenarians who are still driving the roads and "internet" of the alternate ways.

15

The OPEC Monopolies are Arab-Dominated

Oil prices began to decline and by Halloween 2001 had reached down to $21.00 per barrel, the mid-point range. It appears prices are headed for under $10.00 as OPEC struggles to keep prices up while worldwide demand falters. The demand decline is from the recession, something the OPEC nations cannot control. This is why the natural demand cycle dominates all predatory suppliers of products. It seems when the general beliefs reach above 67% for a brief period that the blow-off excess demand is terminated. This seems to apply to most phenomena on earth.

Oil prices rose with the first OPEC increase in 1972-3. It raised retail prices for consumers for food, clothing, transportation, housing and feedstock for the chemical industry by eleven times that of the late fifties creating the great inflation max into February 1982. Then Jimmy Carter, our President before Reagan was caught with the Iran takeover of our embassy in Iran. All personnel in the buildings when the students climbed the walls were imprisoned. Vainly, he attempted a rescue that ended in disaster when his equipment, helicopters and personnel were noted by passing traders who notified the military. It was a disaster waiting for a disaster to happen. Ill conceived and ill pre-pared, Carter caught the blame for the fiasco. He was too involved per-sonally in every action his administration attempted. Interest rates reached their maximum (the cycle again) in February through late summer. Precious metals made their top then and have never seen such highs since. Deflation began and is only now seeking the ultimate low, and we are trying to read the tea leaves through the price of precious metals.

The other controlling factor creating inflation was the implementing of the Great Society of the Johnson Administration in the 1960's. The President funded many new organizations and plans for social change that caused capital providers to raise interest rates rapidly. The cycle seems to have peaked out under President Carter. That was nearly a ten-year period from the low prices of the early 70's when retail prices were steadily rising and then into the crest in spring 1982. It was then that OPEC corralled the oil producers of the world and met in Vienna to restrict production to get prices into the 30 to 40 dollar range out of the $2.00 lows. Thus, inflation with the Oil Bubble began as have other manias among modern man.

The major question might be pertinent to ask at this point. Is the market and economic period from the 1970 lows an aberration, a mania phenomena like the tulip craze or the Mississippi Land bubble that terminated in the market and economic peaks of year 2000?

At this stage there is developing evidence that such was the case. Oil and other forms of energy long monopolized by retailers and OPEC have generated a great deal of technical interest and research into new methods of fueling automobiles and other vehicles as well as energy producers.

During this time the Japanese bought much American real estate, golf courses, prime real estate and used them for tourism from the islands. The bubble began to deflate for Japan around the 1990s and for 11 years now the nation has been and is still liquidating trillions of dollars of its loans made for these purchases.

Argentina was borrowing heavily to modernize industry and it was only in 2001 that the overdeveloped condition caught up with trade monopolies and communication satellite expansion. Trillions of dollars in loans are at risk. President Bush is attempting to assist their rearrangement of financial obligations. If time would improve their situation, then the recovery into late 2002 should relieve much of the economic pressure. Time will tell, the cycle may improve enough to relieve fears.

This time frame appears to have been a major economic bubble around the world. Even Saddam Hussein in Iraq has continued to build castles for himself, although he seems to have little time to enjoy them. We must await the next 18-year low to determine the cycle's validity, around 2008. Major real estate prices may then reach their lows, adjusted for inflation, long-term residents and nation builders!

Iraq has been named as one of the terrorist's states in the State of the Union speech by President George W. Bush. How this will work out in this decade is not readily discerned.

16

Immigration Problems and Coming Change

The appearance of Vicente Fox into the political scene of the southwest and California in particular, changes the game plan of liberals. They have been using the immigrants to bolster their voting blocks for decades.

Presidente Fox of Mexico has asked the dual citizens to return to the homeland to rebuild the Mexican industrial potential into a more powerful economy, with a higher standard of living.

An open border is not likely to ensue. President Fox wants this open border for his country receives millions of dollars sent through channels to the folks back home.

Dual citizenship will not likely be permitted after the next U.S. general election. President Bush has been accused of planning to throw open the borders from the pole to the pole in America. A unilateral America would be incapable of defending itself, as we have known from warfare in the past.

It would be a counter-force compared to China and Europe as it is uniting breaking down borders, races and cultures. Are we going to divvy up the continents among leading races and cultures? This is the current think of many futurists.

If we read our history, not as written by politically correct writers of the nation or region after the clouds of war have cleared, but of the rise and fall of cultures, not of wars or expanding populations/peoples/races running over to another continent or toward a nation that has developed a prosperous way of living, we find a different story exists.

Out of the tortuous life styles, out of the highlands where living is always at the mercy of the bounty of the land, out of the steppes of Asia where the tribesmen of nomadic existence have come together in hordes to plunder, they gather. They begin to merge into a grand army being molded into warrior groups to betray and overtake the witless wanderers, the tourists and other nations.

Where religious zealots come to seek and to impose a belief of power from a god, is perhaps a force beyond their ability to comprehend. But that it does seem to lead them into victory after victory come with the standard bearers of a strange idea. With the mind of peace loving peoples, farmers and traders of life to survive a life they little understand, these marauders convert, kill, rape and destroy all in their path, day after day. This marauder activity seems to be a common trait of mob action too.

The belief is that this is their destiny for their leader claimed it so. Once they find the bounty of the city life and the riches of a culture, they cannot and would not understand, there is only one way to fulfill. It must be destroyed and burned. There are no cultural artifacts that mean anything to peoples who have no knowledge of such achievements as found at seaports, great convergences of trade routes and near the lands that are fruitful and lend themselves to great thoughts and good living. They must be infidels for they cannot be understood in their local tongues. They must be enslaved and forced to do our god's bidding for they are inferior; they are not of our tribe.

Ignorance is a vanity that is not worth rewarding, yet poverty and ignorance dominate the cultures and peoples of the world who have never known anything but what is found in their early years. They have no schools to imitate. Talent is seldom encouraged for their lives are short and filled with ritual, drugs, dogma and dominating leaders who keep them misinformed, uninformed and deliberately used as pawns to be delivered so they may survive.

Those who pause to observe, those who in desperation try to become part of this strange new land learn to speak, work, trade and become part of the culture may become leaders and survivors. Those who fight the system, the masses may not live for long. But those who view the event as an opportunity to achieve and possibly lead the confused out of their simple ways often become fulfilled. Should immigrants, voluntarily or involuntarily under duress, learn the language, the cultural heritage of the new land; they can become part of the great experience. The risk is they will try to return to the homeland, only to be rejected and possibly killed as the new infidel who left their tribe and ventured into another's way of living in the west.

The priests, leaders and family often cast them out. Their lives no longer have meaning. They become lost in the wilderness of new concepts; a religion that has failed them and holds them back, and often their friends reject them when they revert to the old youthful values of the tribes.

The clash of cultures is a time when one repressed nation rises up to destroy the other nation. The language, the religion, and the rituals all hold a people together. Unable to progress in their own language they come to hate the impressing of education and work routines they, as a people or cult, have never seen or understood. Whether it is the five times a day bowing to Mecca by Islam believers, or it is the Catholic trying to understand why Christians left their church, it is the only thing they understand about their god. It is a shallow existence.

They are kept subjugated that way by their elders and clerics who need them to carry out their ambitions. The battle comes when either the clerics have reached autonomous control of their people, they have a military force greater than any of their adversaries, or they feel threatened as a culture. The clerics have autonomous control of their schools and mosques. None dare challenge them. They are expanding their mosques into America, Europe, Africa, Asia, and wherever there is opportunity for the money coming from the Saudi's. It is told we are buying the oil from them. Hence we are funding this Fifth Column in our own land. Our leaders have betrayed us. We must get relief or be engulfed.

Such times are usually near a major crest of a great cycle of nature, one that may have taken a millennium, a time of great climatic vantage where and when the culture has expanded to its limits on the available land. Hitler had his Lebensraum or need for breathing room for his expanding population of Nazi followers.

Genghis Kahn brought his Asian hordes to the middle east and up the river valleys out of the Black and Caspian seas and around the Mediterranean Sea indenturing tribes and slaughtering those unwilling to do yeoman work. Once his lust was fulfilled, leaders were killed, and his armies ravaged by new diseases, the remnants either became local farmers or struggled back to their homelands to die. So, also did the Romans live in the remote ends of the empire once the Caesars of the empire were lost to the Huns and kings that held the lands around their fortresses?

The weakening of the empires comes as the soft life, the inbreeding, the nonsense of non-virtuous living fills the halls of their universities, emporiums and sports centers, auditoriums, the academy and arena their abilities were given over to sport savagery and stress observation without having to participate. The delusion, like television and movies on film staged and scripted were never like the battles of reality. Belief that this was real life activity battling to achieve was at the least fully disarming the public. Radio was communication over vast differences. But TV, movies, DVD and perhaps even the internet verbal exchanges by subject are less than the mental and physical disciplines of acting out ideas of plays and situations in real life. Immigrants, when in overwhelming numbers, tend to destroy a culture, not add to its wealth. It is over-run and debauched by twisted cultural influences of other homelands.

The middle-east oil interests would be a power house of economic growth and creative endeavor with their ability to build great universities to develop their knowledge of physics, mathematics, sciences, philosophies other than their own, space opportunities, agricultural creative practices providing more nutritious foods to their people. The opportunity is endless. They have squandered their religious potential with binding rituals keeping their people ignorant and internally directed. Their early history was a great and growing society. With oil money being used for personal entertainment of the aristocracy and their fine castles, the population that could support a great nation is kept in chains of ignorance. This battle for survival begun by Osama bin Laden and his organization may be the end of Islamic culture, considering the 26,000-year cycle of warming climates appears to have ended.

17

Immigration Trends

A new "Bracero-type" program will probably replace the open border game. New restraints on children born of illegal parents and citizenship should be expected due to this abuse.

Free hospital and medical care, free schooling for their children, food stamps and welfare payments, subsidized housing and other burdens on California taxpayers (also Arizona, New Mexico, Texas and Florida) will only become absent in the economic picture once the liberal socialists are ousted in Sacramento. They will become scarce by 2008. The legislature and Governor Davis approved state tuition rates for illegal resident families if the student spent three years in high school (at state expense) and on going to college will only be charged state rates. There is still something wrong with giving illegals legal rates and privileges as though they were resident native citizens. The property taxpayers are funding these school freeloaders. Why?

Diseases emanating from backward countries are threatening to break out as unmanageable problems like TB, small pox, venereal disease, HIV virus from Africa (40,000 new cases annually) affecting our larger central city populations. Anthrax is not contagious to humans, but can be transmitted if virus is exposed directly to the individual. This could only add to our big city problems and with shrinking taxpayers and increasing illnesses, the medical costs could sky rocket with the tax burden getting even greater than today. The consequences could be devastating to the nation. Must we continue this aberrant course?

President Bush has been "blinking" with border control proposals brought out in talks, interviews and press meetings. This is perhaps one of the greatest problems for this country and by 2008 will become a disaster if not brought sharply under control. He dare not wait much longer before acting to block the flow of undocumented and surreptitiously documented workers into the mainstream. Layoffs continuing into 2003 to 2008 will become hemorrhaging problems.

Excess undocumented labor will be too much for the Administration to ignore anymore. President Bush is attempting to change the policy and favor Mexican labor policies with special privileges for them to work in the U.S.

Unfortunately, this would set up a special class of people with rights even greater than our native born. They could bring relatives equal to eight for each new citizen if given a permanent status. This has hidden the legal immigrant's real family, not two or three but eight making it into a flood. Those devious politicians.

That is a multiplier on our social programs and schools. If Bush will not enforce the border, we have lost anyway so whatever he wants will only make situations worsen. His bias toward his big Hispanic constituency in Texas and his hope to get a larger share of the vote in coming elections could readily destroy the Republican Party voter block. There are no guarantees that the Mexicans will support Republican candidates anyway. The Democratic Party tried buying their favors over the past sixty years and all they want is more, more, more privileges and rights than us.

18

Border Controls

California, at the turn of the millennium, was controlled by Latinos 51% versus. 49%. This includes illegals.

What does this mean to our schools, legislation, health care, and infrastructure? The key question is how many of them are legal voters?

Millions of California residents are "illegals," but in recent elections they were allowed to vote anyway because of Motor Voter registration and the black market in citizenship documents. Estimates are 11 million illegal residents are in California today. Add to that the millions in Texas, Florida, New Mexico, Arizona, Colorado and other agricultural states. Some three million are non-Spanish speaking undocumented residents from China, Pakistan, India, Viet Nam, Afghanistan, Russia, Africa, et al.

The ability of the World Trade Center Islamic destroyers to enter and exit at will at border points, take flying lessons, use credit cards and infiltrate our institutions with sabotage intent is incredible.

We should look at who in our government gutted the CIA, FBI and ATF in the final few decades that permitted these foreign elements to sabotage this nation. Politics aside, the issue can be repeated, and may be duplicated by Iranian, Iraqi, Chinese, Al Qeada (the base) for sabotaging the U.S. with other evil-minded elements to undermine this nation.

During a visit into Romania, the author visited University Square about six months before the dictator was killed by his army on Christmas Eve. These young students and third and fourth generation people under Communist indoctrination and control, milled around the square while a P.A. system blasted out of a second story window. They were trying to fathom the meaning of the single word "freedom."

All their lives had been subjected to instruction as to what they would do, when and how much they would be paid. Theirs had been one of a managed society. They heard, but could not comprehend what "freedom" meant. Their faces screwed up trying to comprehend, as words they had never heard before such as self-responsibility, look for your own job, speak freely about officials, question authority, take care of yourself, go to school where you wish, live where you want to be, read whatever books, magazines, newspapers you like, listen to any radio station you wish, watch any TV program or none. There was usually only one TV and a single radio station available before the dictator was killed. The freedom idea is unknown to many people even today.

How much longer are we going to allow debauchery of the electoral system with liberal and agenda judges and with socialist special interest groups fronting for their votes at election time? How much longer will the bureaucracy be allowed to write the laws, impose them on the public, and then administrate the same laws and all the while the elected officials merely front for their socialist agendas?

We did not elect Senators, Representatives, Governors, Councilmen, Supervisors and dog-catchers to be stooges for liberals and bureaucratic administrators of our country. That is old country thinking, the Chinese way, the French, Russian, German, Islamic and the dictator way of governing.

George W. Bush, our 43rd President started the political change by not allowing the trial lawyers associations to select and pass approval on new judicial appointments. He took the power back to try to get some sense into the judicial system. He has taken power greater than any earlier President. Still his popularity and the trust of the people run 85% with great confidence in his ability to overcome problems he inherited and had imposed on him since taking office. Trust is being given to him that he will do what is right and best for the country. How unique.

Allowing anyone to vote may sound democratic in this republic, but it can also destroy the nation much as the Trojan horse built by Ulysses army of Greek warriors when besieging Troy. They destroyed the ancient Greek city when soldiers inside the wooden horse were then brought inside the walls by the unsuspecting public. They thought it was cute to have a wooden horse to play on. At night the hidden soldiers emerged, opening the gates to the waiting troops. The city was lost when Ulysses returned with the dawn and the residents were killed or enslaved.

Are we going to allow these non-citizens pulsing through our borders the right to take over the political system just because they are here? No other country in the world tolerates the open borders. This is our Achilles Heel, since we are also measuring the risks and comparing the causes of downfall civilizations in our past.

Green cards and easy citizenship were a tool of liberal Democrats to maintain their voter blocks in major cities. That is why they wanted to use the popular vote count versus the Electoral College vote as the law for Federal Elections in year 2000. It is no accident that this Electoral College was put into our Constitution and By-laws. It is there to equalize elections among the states, not just a few big city population votes. These writers knew how people thought and tried to get freebies, even before they arrived in America. Power hungry people use the same old political tools as found in ancient Rome, Greece, China, Japan, India, and in England.

There are those who speak about the coming battle of Blacks versus Hispanics for power to control the big cities, Cincinnati, LA, Seattle, Chicago, New York and even D.C. are ripe for battles. This is one area we hope stays quiet, but we see lots of potential in the battle to divide and conquer for political control by the anarchists, communists and diversity players. They are much the same, and, also aligned with the

ACLU in efforts to divide and conquer the "white" population for socialist enslavement.

There are those who believe that the UN Civil Rights Commission should be paid its $600 million this year (2001). The fact that the U.S. was thrown off the civil rights committee in a secret session in April 2001 showed the intent of Secretary General Kofi Annan. By yielding to pay the UN back dues, it would discredit the U.S. and would be acquiescing to their demands. Nearly half was ordered withheld by the State Department, which gives some wiggle room in negotiations.

It is said by some reporters that paying the bill would signal the end of our independence and loss of our freedom, granting the power of our freedoms to the UN. We must not let that happen and we must get out of the UN now.

19

Threat to U.S. Security is from Within

Our non-documented and falsely documented relatively new citizens brought in to vote for Democratic Party candidates mainly over the years are not loyal in the same way to this new homeland as we used to be with our freedom-seeking forefathers.

In the Communist China government pilot downing event of our surveillance craft in spring 2001, many of the Chinese receiving SSI payments and their families criticized President Bush and wanted him to apologize to the Chinese President. Chinese-Americans called into talk radio show hosts in San Francisco stating their anger at the U.S. Nearly 90% of callers were being loyal to the old homeland.

Should these recipients be asked to state in writing their loyalty to the U.S.? Somewhere we will have to draw the line and gather up the questionable ones and return them to their homelands. China has many military espionage agents planted in U.S.A. Many Arabs are planted to "sleep" until needed in the Mosques and the villages dominantly held for the culture of their past. They are not becoming Americanized and learning English in many instances and many are just waiting for orders to act.

Latinos have many among us who refuse to speak English and return to their homeland regularly while they receive food stamps, subsidies, schooling and health care for their children. Loyalty is not found sufficient because of Uncle Sap giving them the freebies.

Many of these loyalists to foreign leaders should be removed from our society without the benefit of again returning for any form of life here. They have not earned this right nor pledged loyalty to the U.S. Their actions belie their comments.

We now have fifth-column communities in every major city.

Our William J. Clinton Administration, 42nd President, sold the secrets of our umbrella in missile guidance shields to the Chinese for a handful of silver coins.

Traitors to the U.S. have not been dealt with properly even when they gave secrets to enemies for pennies to enhance their own desire for security. We have not punished them! They should be. Cases from the Afghan war will proliferate and divide us, if we do not draw the line. Jane Fonda retains that image even today as a liar and saboteur. Just because our wars are no longer declared by Congress, our modern Benedict Arnolds can get away without paying the price that Whittiker Chambers did.

There is no social, political or physical threat to any U.S. traitor—he can be kept in prison, nothing else. Why should any traitor fear death, punishment or imprisonment in this country? Few are caught and fewer of them imprisoned.

Lawyers have gotten them off the hook and then they proved their guilt by running to their foreign friends and lands to live in peace and quiet, many getting SSI and retirement benefits from U.S.

The apathy among voters that permits the election of a dictator or popular leader is one group that hopes the good times will continue once the new leader's promises appear to be correcting problems that have demoralized their own community of interest.

Few feel their votes count. Is apathy with a 40% turnout projected in 2002 elections? Probably, that is about as good as it will get until the threats drop on us again from some source.

There is only one solution to stop the worst of the internal sabotage. When it is a neo or actual treasonous act, a quick public execution should follow. It should not take years of wrangling and political "spin" of the defense and the press to discern intent and action to be taken. Change the rules for declaring wars, like the President does since Congress is so full of the multi-cultural special interests.

The cry of the weak and self-serving cults may readily say that the penalty is too severe and they will quickly demonstrate in the streets hoping to change the court's decision. This only shows how weak and infiltrated we've become in law enforcement of criminals of all ages, with treasonous political intent and often profiled to some common ethnic origins.

We do not know the extent of the infiltrator activities in the FBI, CIA, ATF (Alcohol Tobacco and Firearms), National Security Council and agencies as well as the local constabulary. We do know that it is within these next few years that major overhauls of these three agencies also will have to come to purge the doubt about their ability to protect the nation. Having seen the abuse of their agencies in the past decade from Ruby Ridge, Waco and conflict of interests with the Chinese including our top secret nuclear research facilities, public confidence has fallen to nearly 50% of the voters.

With illegal aliens jumping into our harbors, climbing our fences and fording the rivers of our borders, how much "willpower" is there left among the voters to survive and protect this nation against these villainous groups? Our land is ripe for the picking.

20

Where the Great Risk Abounds

The greatest loss is with the highly placed elected and appointed agency leaders who seek power at any price and give away anything to get the funds and backing for their potential dictatorship.

We were lucky that Al Gore and his power-hungry followers, communists and socialistic thinkers and revisionists, the "government knows best" philosophers and those who would do the central planning for all to follow, were soundly rejected in election year 2000.

They will attempt to recover in 2002 & 2004 and take-over Congress again. Will they succeed? We will have to block their liberal action at every turn and opportunity. Into the next election, little creative reconstruction of the economy will take place. It will attempt to right itself, but by election time in 2002, the trouble resumes by sudden social problems or a sabotage action.

Shades of Stalin, and the communists, who are still in control seem to have spread their philosophy among the post WW II generation. It was only a little over a decade ago, after the end of the Russian Communist Confederation broke down, that the Berlin Wall was destroyed by free men of western Germany. Everyone inside the wall seemed to want out and to circumvent it or climbed over the barrier to freedom. Communism had lasted for over 100 years. We still find that communists and socialists cannot be re-educated. It would seem that this malaise of social dependency on big government is in the screen of paternity of their minds, the soil where they live or the very air they breathe infecting the entire value system they purport is greatest.

They failed miserably to achieve economic freedom, equality of citizens and political freedom for their people. The fraud has been exposed! Yet, they persist! Once a communist, always a communist! Perhaps it will come to the old slogan "The only good communist is a dead communist!"

Still, some 20,000,000 American voters believe in Central Planning, as we seem to have derived our views from socialist elitist thinking. They are not real communists but are approving of communists and their ways. It sounds like they are communists, too, because they support these deviants. This is the dominant theory taught in our schools and universities of higher learning up till now. There are clues that some universities are changing concepts.

This is why the next revolution will focus on purging the miscreants that fill the minds of innocent young trusting students to get the stuff that is good and real, only to discover it is a fraud, a slick paint job over damaged bodies, a false god for man to follow.

It is the absence of having national heroes around to model our lives after and goals to achieve even greater things for mankind. That is the social failure. Is it a mental scourge to which our educational system may succumb? Is it the golden calf of false leadership?

21

Anarchist Day of Infamy

The May Day (1st) celebration around the world is perhaps the greatest example today of irrational and irrelevant thinking prevalent in world society today. Can you imagine a world without the UN, America, England, Iran, Iraq, Israel, China, Australia, Japan, Ireland and other countries that we see and read about in the news?

Anarchists are by definition a society without a leader, tough, gang run, undisciplined roaming opportunists who destroy what they do not want, kill wantonly, take what they need, pillage, rape and burn, wasting the work of freedom-loving and proud people who were building a society greater than themselves.

It is like opening the prison doors and turning the hardened criminals loose on a working orderly society without police or military personnel to protect us, and without real bullets in their guns, perhaps rubber bullets as the maximum firepower.

Against the law and order bunch is the ruthless, possibly deranged or amoral person with great killing skills taking whatever he wants from anyone, anywhere, anytime. There is no punishment left for him (her) for they have little to lose if caught. They are rape, pillage, burn and torture all wrapped in one personal package.

They are as close to the anti-Christ concept, the devil of biblical beliefs, those things that are negative to all who believe in man as an extension of God, the great creator of life. They are nihilistic, self-centered, arrogant, devious, without redeeming concepts and are the bane of life as we know it. Their word is false. Those the author has met were totally unscrupulous, liars, had amoral if any values and for a dollar would kill anyone.

With no moral values, they are like wild animals roaming the lands imitating citizens with false promises and outright lies to destroy all semblance of society, including their own. They hate Capitalism, Communism, socialism and any organized work ethic, any successful practice in creating a better society. One of the most creative ventures in man's history can fall into rubble in minutes when attacked by an anarchist.

The seeds of destruction are always born within the framework of a society's institutions. It is the virus that kills, weakens or subverts objectivity. Every society breeds its own destruction element by tolerating deviants that enjoy destroying. They are the characters in movies, stories and headlines because they are not like 99% of us. We are entertained by their stories. What kind of stories should we expect from Hollywood media?

It would be difficult for mankind to create anything more destructive than a roaming band of anarchists carrying an atom bomb around in a pickup through our cities and countryside.

Russia, Andrews reminds us, was managed and controlled for many years by a Communist Party membership of less than 1% of their population. Being "card carrying" members of the Communist Party was a free ride to whatever one wanted. These members lived in the mansions of the kings and were seldom disciplined for abuse of power. They were the new type of kings, reigning as long as they espoused the socialist concepts that "big brother knows best." Unable to view life from any other perspective these believers live a life frustrated beyond reason. That makes them dangerous.

They cannot accept the fact that no one knowingly will risk his capital to fund a false idea or work project where the capital is dissipated to the employees and none to the creators of that wealth.

This is the worm theory of life: Bore into the good fruit and eat the heart out of the gift of life to satisfy your own greed and desire to live. It is inborn. Moths and worms have little respect for our food and clothes, but are food for the birds and bats of earth. When they are near the bottom of the food chain, we use insecticides. Not too bad a place to start spraying our vermin.

Infestations of grain come and go along with viruses like the potato wilt that destroyed the Irish food crop. It is the destruction of many cattle with the Hoof & Mouth disease in England and some local areas of Europe. A virus is moving westward out of the blue grass Kentucky fields where horses are aborting, threatening the racing and breeding industry. HIV virus is another type of disease that flares up as the plague did in Europe many years ago killing nearly half the population within a few years bringing on the dark ages of survival. There will always be another type of plague to strike us when we get too numerous and too cocky about our success stories. Nature gets perverse when our beliefs get too outrageous among leaders…that man controls all.

We must be vigilant or we could replicate this dangerous idea easily. The concepts exuded through the evil minds of communists are not easily destroyed or replaced with creative ventures. This is one of the threats to world salvation from ignorance that man may observe during this next century. Communism is for redistribution of wealth created by non-communist peoples.

There will be conflicts and open street battles often in alignments with anarchists, which will attempt to destroy this society. How well we accept the challenge in the battle for survival will determine whether this or any other nation will long survive this and similar anti-social ideas that loots all that in man's history has been produced in thousands of years.

Within these next ten years, some more scandals and risks to our safety will be revealed. Perhaps the damage being done today will be too great to allow this nation to recover more than temporarily.

Our security is a sieve for sorting out only the big lumps while the real secrets are slipped past and around the border guards then given to our enemies by our own people. Be eternally vigilant.

That threat to our security is irresponsibility and the ability of the elected and powerful in key political positions to siphon away the life-blood of our technical research, the education of our youth and the health of the working public.

Meaningless slogans and jingoism have become the language of the politician and the journalist alike who slouch through the hard decisions and make use of platitudes with ill defined meanings for their rule of law.

It is the rule of Constitutional Law, defined and implemented by hard and honest work that makes this system survive! It is being subverted daily. We must block them wherever we can.

22

Evidence of Big Changes Coming

The evidence is coming in almost hourly as the epitome of recent social achievements by ecologists, environmentalists, socialists, nihilists, One World UN enthusiasts, dictators, extremists and historical regressive vandal-thinking beings. Their false premises are imploding as their overkill efforts cause the public to turn against them.

Some will disagree with these conclusions, but everyone who loses a battle or a court case rationalizes and blames another or then calls the setback "temporary."

When the early evidence became noticed that Global Warming was another false god of the poorly informed and the somewhat twisted concepts of life, which appeared in 2000, most would not believe it. The whole idea was adopted by would-be scientists jumping on the band-wagon to get funding for their political and social agendas. Not knowing the causes of global warming, how can ecologists and scientists even know if the climate is abnormal today? We spend millions daily on false ideas. So, why should this idea prove to be different?

It has created Junk Scientists who often have failed to justify their conclusions with facts repeatable by other investigators, which is cause for rejecting their premises. We have many scientists who have been trained by University Professors with political agendas they developed since the end of WWII and in the Great Depression when socialism was embraced and social planning was embodied into the domestic structure as idealism reappeared. President Woodrow Wilson, (28th, serving from 1913-21) in WW I was fond of the socialist principles and supported the League of Nations. The League was a failure too. It was the result of 200 years of socialist philosophy in the 1700's as the industrial revolution evolved. It was finally proven to be as ineffective in real life as efforts to improve social programs are now being de-funded.

In some areas of science, just like in religion, there are forbidden ideas that continue to dominate man's experiences. "Jobs for every-one," as though everyone wants a nine-to-five way of life and no more food shortages as well as birth to death medical care. Slowly, these areas are being eroded and the facts exposed. Science will now have to begin to change and become more objective, concerned less with agenda and more with new leaders, tighter philosophical ideas of what science can and will do, who open the great 21st Century living to greater new ideas and technologies never dreamed of by philosophers of the last millennium.

Perhaps some one-third of the population would not support this concept, being liberal in thinking. But, about 16% of the population voted with the socialists until the turn of the millennium. We now find a shrinking populist liberal movement and many are voting more con-servatively. The Bush 43rd Presidency is a mix of some conservative thinking and goals but many agencies are and still filled with liberals who want open borders, birth to death health care and guaranteed jobs for everyone.

Even PBS (Public Broadcasting System) is showing less intransi-gence and programming giving a new perspective as their public fund-ing seems to be slowing. New thinking is appearing.

Strove Talbot, one of the Bush inner circles, is opposed to closed borders. That is pure communism in the reverse. Communism in Europe kept the borders closed to keep the citizens enslaved and in. In the U.S., we can't keep them out because of the "free lunches" in health care, minimum wages, schools, cheap home and auto loans, food stamps, subsidized housing and greater protection of their rights than of the natural born citizen.

If Steve Fox (Mexican Presidente) doesn't take advantage of us now to subvert the Treaty of Guadalupe and take over Norte California again, he won't get a better chance. Even Governor Gray Davis is supporting his ambitions following his own socialist party line. The last chance is after the Crash of 2008 ends.

Even the opponents of this massive change weakly thought they had won a staying rear guard action with the vicious electioneering and subversion with much of our liberty loving tools such as election 2000 procedures and vote buying in Florida. In the end, battles may be won by the use of the last pitchfork or rifle shot that strikes its mark demoralizing the enemy fatally. The army ground troops still must hold the cities and roads, if we don't use them for more than distributing food to the poor.

Unable to mount a new political front against the opposing "Conservative" power now in the White House, the war has to end. There are usually skirmishes with recalcitrant elements, which have failed to get the message that the end has come for liberal and socialistic programs. We, as a society, will have to deal with those organized elements, which cannot accept the changes that inevitably follow after the final battle has been fought. A purge will come to end the harassment and sabotage of our institutions.

We are still fighting the battles of the Civil War, (War Between the States), with flag dispersions, political alignments, demands for reparations by the freed slave remnants who are still slaves in their own minds, building monuments to the fallen soldiers and the rewriting of history about the wished for facts.

History is always written by the victors, no matter how the fight was won. The events of the times dictate what is relevant. Those who oppose the line of thinking that follows new leadership may never be able to present their point of view. In private conversations, some will claim a fraud, but most people like to follow the winners and put down the losers. The defeated remnants can only pout and become the loyal opposition attempting to sabotage the works of the winners.

Even the attempt of recent months by Bob Kerry of Nebraska to rewrite the meaning and interpretation of the Viet Nam (police action) conflict, with the awarding of bronze stars for events, and interpretations by aged observers caught in their Nam village. Those who gave the marching orders claimed the orders were mistakenly written. Guilt trips for doing the jobs assigned by those legislature based politicians with a safe haven in Washington make the revision of values and taking the events of the times "out of context" to gain re-election popularity in today's society. Every few years these stories pop up and feed the media, often as a diversion from some more important event.

It is becoming more transparent every day to the public that such ploys are rear guard actions (retreating troops) by a losing concept of organized social life in America and that big government can solve all social problems. It is over. When will the "nearly seniors group" quit trying to change the past?

The conflict was over political issues and whether the evils of social-ism/communism would prevail or a seeming alternate noted as self-direction by freedom-loving peoples who would turn the elections. The vicious attempts to gain control of our Constitutional Republic since the undeclared wars after WWII are nothing more than sore los-ers who cannot understand that man does poorly when he is placed in a mental straight-jacket of economic and social thinking. He has nowhere to go but down as he fights the system just to survive. Islam and religiously controlled nations keep themselves on short tethers with rituals for poverty and ignorance of what causes man to want to survive, achieve and prosper. They destroy the hunger of young men and women to be anything more than their parents or their peers. It is still a defective religion no matter how many prophets have had dreams of grandeur and world domination.

Christianity has its faults and points that need to be clarified, but over the years they too have gaps. Ancient religions emphasize the gods and have various names depending on the age of the culture, its location north or south of the equator, east and west of the more populated lands. Archaeologists are finding them almost everywhere in more remote regions and in mountain abodes.

A number of specific events and court decisions show the shift is going to be rapid and sure in the next decade for the retainable conservative values of society.

It happened again. Dr. Spock is being downgraded. A group of research psychologists from Berkeley, CA. (University of California) have concluded that spanking a child does not inhibit or give a social stigma for being spanked. This was reported at the Institute of Human Development, presented by Elizabeth Owens and Diana Baumrind, at the San Francisco meeting of the American Psychological Association by the Associated Press August 25, 2001.

The sting is all that remains and the memory of being disciplined with a mild spanking. There is a reward for discipline in that the child remembers the pain and abides by the discipline of the school into adolescence. The "red zone" of 4 to 7% of the parents who disciplined frequently and impulsively, with verbal, paddle, hitting in the face or torso, shaking or throwing were found to experience anxiety or depression in later years. The majority of parents used moderate methods of discipline. The carrot is far more effective in discipline and training procedures. But, outside of animal husbandry, who teaches it for the parents of tomorrow's parents?

Whether the children who received heavier doses of discipline and then who were anxious and depressed in later years would have likely been troubled anyway was not mentioned. Expect more research in this direction now.

We go through these stages in child raising, capital punishment, getting traffic tickets from overhead intersection cameras, and court cases settled for multi-millions of dollars by a vengeful group of jurors and their liberal judges. Yes, liberal judges who seem to be out of their realm of authority in legal decision-making punishment.

Then there is the educational system that places emphasis on job security of the teachers and administration above the student learning basic information for survival and creation. Then, there is freedom to indulge in sex as more important in any society for the personal expression of the individual person, when the taboos are meant for the prevention of epidemics of social diseases and the structure of the family. Yes, and they are meant for the protection of the children from slavery as is still found in many lands, and the lack of discipline to direct their lives into constructive channels.

In a recent story by Newsday reporter Edward A. Gargan on rural China, observes that the people are having a resurgence of folk religions as a way of communicating. Rural political power and authority are becoming a practice after the Cultural Revolution which destroyed the many small temples of the nation. Superstitious practices and folk religion are virtually ignored while the Falun Gong, a quasi-Buddhist exercise and spiritual sect has been suppressed. In Sgaabxu alone some 1,300 temples have been built in the past decade. The poorest temples such as those of the Black Dragon Pool are supplanting the authority of the Communist Party, like being a small country, an empire unto itself.

23

Climate Myopia: Global Warming?

Common sense among the readers of magazines, newspapers and listeners to TV and talk radio has reached different conclusions of global warming than do the environmentalists and news columnists.

With so much history forgotten or never noted, and so little found in the laboratory dish and apparatus in the search for facts or truth, it seems that archaeologists are proving that a global lifestyle concept is no more than another scam on the public.

Having dug through layers of earth over ancient cities and living sites, the ruins exhibit layer-upon-layer of evidence. Climate changes do occur over thousands of years. Man adapts to the changes by living nearer to waters, digging wells, digging cisterns or living near an oasis with underground reservoirs. We drill for deep-water basins to supplement rain shortfall.

In the sixth and 17th centuries it was bitterly cold in Europe. In the ninth and 13th centuries it was warm enough to support citrus in England, wines in Norway and Sweden, bulbs and flowers in Holland on the mud flats.

There have been ice ages and it is believed to have been as many as five different ages of man who have come and gone. Our climate science models are more hearsay and junk scientists abound to justify their grants and wages in support of their University or institution of higher learning. Even NASA encourages these unproven sciences and even they help provide budget for research. We do a lot of useless scientific studies that no one ever hears about or is ever catalogued should someone else want funding grants to replicate them.

24

Confirming the Shift to Conservatism

Election reversals often signal that the new age is coming! It isn't the Age of Aquarius like the musical show intones.

In Israel, Barak got 40.5% Sharon 59.5% of the votes on Feb 6, 2001 election, confirming a turn of the times to stronger disciplines of government and negotiations.

Palestine leader Yassir Arafat is aging quickly, and in his absence could trigger a major shift in the Middle East soon. He is ill! Fomenting hatred for Israel, teaching the children to hate instead of learning skills and developing the mind, importing arms from Iraq/Iran/China to kill Israel citizens signals a long-term problem in Middle East politics. Working against Israel is the shrinking of aquifers in the region. This had given them prosperity in the past 60 years. Society cringes with droughts. The population growth has consumed the water available to supply the new residents.

What will happen when the leadership changes? It will give a new political direction probably, but it will also take years to overcome hate inbred in the Palestinians and Islamic students being indoctrinated and who are seeking their own homeland. How they react to the coming new age will give us many clues about how peace in the region will be achieved in the future.

In Canada, we already have the conservative Premier. Like Vicente Fox in Mexico, the conservatives are arriving. Don't trust this Fox with

NAFTA privileges! His attitude is extreme liberal and his actions are anti-north American while he talks like a conservative. France, typically, elected a new socialist leader this year. Count them as confused! Historically, they cannot be defended. Will they ever become defenders of their homeland?

The Japanese leader was replaced in April 2001 as their economy was collapsing much as ours was under William Jefferson Clinton when he left office to find his new legacy. They are struggling to right their economic ship in Japan.

Tony Blair in England is hanging by a thread and was reelected. Unusual, but he is changing his views to more conservative to keep his job. William Hague, British Conservative Party Leader wanted lower fuel taxes, to keep the Kyoto agreement like Europe wants, lower cost of big government by four billion pounds (of silver), and a new system of government budget financing of agencies. He lost! His was tailored toward conservative, but barely. Charles Kennedy, British Liberal Democratic Party Leader, sought more social programs and a bigger government participation in the lives of the citizens. He lost too. William Hague had the moxie to defeat Tony Blair. He didn't. Blair was reelected but with a low voter turnout. Caution will have to be his game. Things are not going well on the island. Resistance to the European central control of economies is not popular among the voters. The economic crash may cause Blair to pull in his socialist horns for now.

Japanese market and banking systems collapsed into '89 lows. Interest rate is ½% today (negative 2½%) over borrowing costs of the government, and is likely to go almost to zero in their attempt to rejuvenate their industrial base. This is comparable to the U.S. crash in '29 when stock margin rates were low (10%) and almost anything qualified for a loan to invest in the stock market. On June 27, 2001 FRB lowered U.S. discount interest rates another .25%. By late August they were down to 3%—just where the low occurred 37 years ago. That is the 37-year cycle again, or worse still since we observe the economic weakness into 2008. In December 2001, they leveled off at 1.25%.

Changes will follow in a desperate attempt to still the recession and turn it into recovery quickly. It will be a chore for the new Japanese leader as will George Bush in the U.S. Theirs is a serious economic condition since their excesses were similar to ours 70 years ago.

25

Crash of 2008

The cost of government has risen since 1950 from around 20% to over 30% in 1999. That's a 50% increase in about the same number of years—1% per year. Regulations and reports are another form of taxation including the 35% added cost to labor contracts when using any government funds to build or modify projects and facilities.

Then there are additives to motor fuel to minimize smog that adds to the cost of living, but are not included in the calculation. Then there are fines for passing through yellow lights where camera-ready controls are positioned, fines for speeding, or too slow, maximum fines where construction is occurring, fines for airlines (who pass it onto ticket buyers), and fines against corporations for minor infractions (also passed on). We all know that the consumer pays these fines, not the company. Postal rate increases, minimum wage increases, surcharges for energy, port taxes, landing fees, license fees, etc.

It is just the way the system has begun to operate, plus taxes collected at all levels seem to total to around 45% or more of GDP (gross domestic product).

The 2001 estimates are for Federal Taxes $2.14 trillion, state and local taxes $1.14 trillion, Federal Regulations $866.71 billion, state regulations $552.07 billion for a total of $4.57 trillion versus. GDP estimates of $10.0 trillion. Source: *Americans for Tax Reform*. Note: It was about 1946 when the GDP reached $1.billion per year. Only 54 years ago, the cost of living was about 8% of what it is today.

Looked at another way, the number of days the average taxpayer works for the government reached 187 days in 1999. That's 51.23% of the work days.

In the 1950 era, the number was under two to three months and considered cheap since we had all the war costs to carry prior to that. What happened that all these increases came in bundles? It began in the mid-1960's, with the Great Society programs under President Johnson (36th). Look at the burgeoning national debt after 1965.

Minor tax cuts of 1/3rd for the under $26,000 income payers into this first decade makes the benefit seem fair. We will have to wait and see how it really works out. This is a mere pittance and merely a token since most of it is in 2010. It has a sunset clause of 2011. When do we get a tax break?

With Senator Jim Jeffords (age 67) Republican from Vermont switching to Independent, the 50-50-vote in the Senate has threatened the Republican power base. He was always a liberal, poorly a Republican. Unless something happens to change the balance into 2002, Minority Leader Tom Daschle ND, Marxist all the way, took over from Trent Lott of Mississippi as leader. Never thought Lott had much backbone, but lots of pork and log rolling skills.

The new Senate President changed all the committee chairmen to Democrats. He left the nation with sand in the gears. Still the VP can break the ties with his vote and may have to do it frequently until election 2002 puts new blood in the Senate. What happened to the joint agreement on running the Senate with Daschle? Gone! It was only a liberal ploy to hold some strings.

If the conservative side of politics has really turned away from liberal, big government thinking, this spring's nominations in California and many other state primaries will show the evidence. The confirmation will come in November '02 elections. Look for the conservatives to sweep local, state, federal and city elections.

26

Educational Failures and Changes Needed

Not very many years ago, about 55 of them, California had some of the finest public educational institutions in the nation. Today it is nearly at the bottom of the list. It looks like Arkansas and California are vying for bottom. Similar indoctrination programs have been put in place at ivy-league and many eastern colleges and universities.

One going against the trend is Hillsdale College in Hillsdale, Michigan 49242. They claim they take no government subsidies, grants, or contracts and no student tuition from government. Consequently, they can manage their curriculum with no interference by government social programs, agenda, preferences, standards and course material. They teach liberal arts, always have it is believed, so that graduates learn to think for themselves. They give grants in aid to needy students.

They publish a monthly newsletter called IMPRIMIS, because "Ideas Have Consequences" with 1.1 million readers. Their endowment is increasing rapidly whereas many other colleges are fighting to hold their supporters and alumni. Universities are getting stiff competition. There will be a rash of them refusing government funds in the next ten years marked by changing standards. Higher levels of grades are coming from the private sector.

The liberal California Legislature is one of the last in the nation that has not become anti-liberal. It does not want to approve the voucher system to allow any competition in the public schools. Give us four more years of this kind of leadership and the voucher system will be a natural as indoctrination becomes endemic. The entire concept of liberalism seems to be coming apart, even the taking of lands for environmental purposes. The California Coastal Commission was declared unconstitutional but decision is being appealed to Supreme Court.

Andrews projects a collapse of liberal legislator control and social programs into 2008 economic lows. California will again become conservative. It should be evident of the turn by 2004.

What could possibly have happened in Sacramento that the house of cards could be shaken so readily? Big Labor unions have backed the liberal plank and have their own house to protect, the Teacher Union's control the legislature. It has been a union state for many years. Even the issue over how to solve the 2000 energy crisis revolved around the unions taking more control.

Andrews sees a new legislature power base for Conservative action in 2002, 2004, 2006 and finally into 2008. A new California Governor, and vouchers for public schools in the next general election. Tax cuts are not likely what with the energy crisis taking the cash to keep a citizen revolt from beginning. If the new legislature can enact sane and objective laws then the energy shortfall may be cured and will permit a tax cut. Governor Gray Davis signed energy and gas contracts at peak prices. This has destroyed the state's surplus and has forced the replacement of 0.25% increase in the sales tax. The state will be bitter before the next general election.

Many of the liberal states like Connecticut, the Dakotas, Florida, Illinois, Maine, Massachusetts, Minnesota, New Hampshire, New York, Vermont, Washington, and Wisconsin will whittle down their liberal agenda and elected legislators and the strength of the liberal vote. Their strength is not as great as their newspapers suggest.

Nearly three-fourths of the states have dominant Republican legislatures and governors already. Expect the liberal states remaining to become isolated from Federal programs involving funding and social programs. These states, living off the rest of us taxpayers will change their leadership simply from lack of needed funds.

27

Election 2000, a Cultural Turn Signal

A turn signal! Florida squeaked through to show the turn of the great cycle of 26,000 years was valid. The result is expected to be a climate cooling condition slowly lowering the heat levels, not more global warming. Such things start slowly, accelerate then terminate in a bang with an iceberg. This is only one of a series of events showing great changes are in process.

The philosophical changes are noticed already. Liberal socialistic programs now seem to fall on deaf ears, their plans being fraught with weakness and misdirection. Liberal voters listened and then turned their backs on the liberal politicians. Conservative Democratic Party elected leaders are now siding with the Republican leadership. They fear a total rejection of their beliefs could follow in 2002 and their political clout could be eliminated in just 18 months.

They have much to worry about because they overplayed their hands and tried to smash all Republican and opposition to keep their socialist goals. Tom Daschle, Hillary Clinton and Teddy Kennedy are attempting to push their agendas quickly, now that they are in control. The test of the trend will be whether they can garner enough votes to support them. As of year-end they were stalemated.

Still, Tom Jeffords of Vermont on May 24, 2001 jumped out of the Republican Party and went into the Independent party, not the Democratic Party. He is a liberal, socialist inclination, and probably will run for Vermont governor by 2006. This left the Democratic Party with a 50 to 49 majority. Minor shifts can easily control the Senate in spite of the socialist and socialization of the medical profession planning agenda.

Independents have no party support. Jeffords, a closet Democrat, will work with the Democrats. Power went to the liberal Democrats with Tom Daschle moving in as Majority Leader. This power can go back and forth between major parties as others switch or resign. Nothing is going to be gained by individuals switching. Voting blocks are more likely to dominate the politics of the Senate.

28

Energy Prices: Cause and Effect

Years of unjust persecution of businesses by ecologists, the regulatory agencies and socialists elected from the pool of indoctrinated youth of the 60's, who have assumed control of the state, has poisoned the atmosphere for new business to set up shop in California.

The California Energy Crisis took a great toll on the economy. The other 49 states may have laughed at Governor Davis, but, since the same philosophy is expressed by state PUC regulators as his, he remains. Many of them experienced the same rip-off through the pump price or the utility rate structure. Vigilance is not something turned on one day and not the next.

Nowhere else has the shortfall struck so hard in the 12 months since summer of 2000 than in California and the drought-stricken Northwest and Southwest. The crisis caused the big state to sap the energy from the Northwest power dams (also with drought conditions) to the Texas power grid most recently with its many new generators; it was the last straw. It was not repeated elsewhere in the country in any other state. So, it had to be politically driven. How could leaders get so stupid so fast?

It is an opportunity for residents and businessmen of other states to protect their turf and to avoid the California error. They can profit by selling into California because of lower production costs.

One can only say that the crisis shortfall of electricity and natural gas and motor fuel was from bungling the 1996 so called deregulations putting a cap cn retail prices while letting the wholesale spot price swing freely. It was politically irrational to attempt to float the retail price of energy and gas.

Anyone who has traded futures knows that the spot market is volatile and full of quicksand traps. It was also an opportunity for other energy suppliers to milk the Californian of his prosperity from the high tech industry.

Having shut down many of the smaller energy generators and municipal plants in the name of efficiencies, even hydro plants were not allowed to modernize and many were forced to be sold to new owners (out of state, of course), over the past five years because of environmental rationalizing and political intrigue of the conservationists. This includes the Sierra Club, Earth Liberation Front, Radical Greens, and coastal and land use fronts, where there were no preserves.

New permits were almost non-existent for over a decade from the 80's, while many marginal generators with minor smog problems were permitted only limited use.

Shutting down generation capacity for ecological reasons of owls, fish, snails and frogs and on occasional smoggy days when fog hung low in the west, showed how little objective thinking was taking place among the legislatures and those appointed to Public Utility Commission offices throughout the country. California was one of the worst culprits. During the winter of 2000-01 marginal diesel generators created higher smog levels and became a cry for the environmentalists to strike back against the trend to lower standards to accommodate the public need.

The time has come for the objective changes to begin.

The flag went up for the utility companies (particularly PG&E and S.C. Edison International) domestic suppliers of energy as the decade began with no new plants in approval stage or in construction within the state. The costly environmental and construction standards imposed even after approvals were made, was forcing these utility companies to buy more power from outside sources. Then, in 1996 they were required to buy at the "spot market" price. Note the similarity of buying oil from OPEC on the spot markets to cover regional shortfalls. Even the oil from the national reserve could not be refined into motor fuel, under Clinton, and it was shipped overseas at great profit for the bidders. Many of these nouveau oil merchants were political buddies of the liberal pols and who never even attempted to supply local refineries. There was no capacity available, it was claimed.

Their only choice was to divert their capital to other states or countries so they set up new umbrella corporations now known as PG&E and Edison International with headquarters outside the State of California. Local facilities became separate corporations or subsidiaries with limited capital exposure.

Much of their working capital was siphoned off into these new corporations then invested in foreign nations and in new facilities within the U.S.A., but out of control of the California environmentalists and the state legislature. This put their generating assets beyond the liberal socialist legislators dominating the industry at the millennium turn.

How much do you suppose these international companies actually overcharged their own subsidiaries in California during the crisis? The evidence is there and the Governor has it. Will he be willing to use it as a thrust to destroy private energy investment?

On "May 12, 2001 it was reported by the Los Angeles Times, that in May 2000 California power plants have been shutting down—purportedly for repairs and maintenance—at rates two, three and four times higher than before, according to figures made public by the state Energy Commission."

"The figures, posted on the commission's web site this week, provided new evidence to those who believe the generators have been manipulating the state's electricity market by creating an artificial shortage." It reached a peak in April when the amount offline was 350% greater than in April 2000. There were 14,990 megawatts, about one-third of the state's total needs. At the same time the cost increased from $30 per megawatt hour last April 2000 to well over $1500 later in the year. In May 2001 it reached $2000 a megawatt hour (one megawatt hour = about 750 homes).

The long-term solution plan was to create competition by allowing suppliers to contract with large users, and to distributors and consumers alike. The risk of losses through Chapter 11 reorganization bankruptcies to themselves as well as suppliers in other states threatened the entire national energy policy (as practiced) that was piecemeal throughout the country.

Retired personnel in the industry depend on those dividends to pay the rent. If the utility was bankrupt, they were penniless and without dividends. Many retirees had stock in the utility companies nationwide and could well get caught in the collapse that could readily ensue in other states. Enron, symbol ENE, had manipulated prices, cooked the books, and as it became known; their stock dropped to under a dollar. Retirees and employees lost their stake in company stock and in the retirement plans. Problems at the SEC?

Bringing down the entire system was what was happening under the Davis Administration and the state legislature. No one wanted that, but Governor Davis seemingly could only find solutions that destroyed the industry and eventually put the state into the energy and distribution business, thinking like socialists usually do that which they know best.

The unions were great supporters of this same thinking for they would then be able to control the grid and plants through their state unions and force extraordinary pay increases as well as soft work rules. They would be able to fund and help elect future liberal socialists to maintain their power base. That means they would take all the ordinary business profits and set up subsidy games to milk the ratepayers even more than in 2000-01.

This plan seems to be going against the new era trend of deregulation and greater competition. So there must be another solution. Later you will read about that possibility. A new Field Poll gives us 59%

favoring Nuclear Energy use for California, a decided reversal. What happened to the socialization schemes?

29

Gasoline, Food and Energy Shortfall

Growth of population and the high tech industry in the San Francisco Bay area as well as the Seattle area has increased industrial demand for stable energy sources. Southern California has a large share of the new industrial programs that lead world communications.

Roaming blackouts by the California Public Utilities Commission (when 5% reserves were reached) shut down the Bay area several times in winter months of 2001 causing expensive idleness to production and internet service operations.

To restart electronic manufacturing plants meant dumping the in-process product that was ruined, resetting the software programs, equipment and quality control.

Gray Davis became a nasty word among the liberal boomers of the bay area and the region. They were fast becoming conservatives over-night because of the pound foolishness of the administration of the PUC and the state legislators. Ill thought out programs emanated hourly from Sacramento.

Gasoline with additives that were polluting the water supplies was becoming another big issue but no legislative decisions seemed to be forthcoming that solved the problems, only big talk. Unable to lead, Davis is counted out for reelection, even though he will remain governor until the next election. Like Clinton, nobody seems to want to upset the apple cart. It has been a long time since California was any-thing but in the pocket of Big Labor and liberal social planners.

When will this kind of socialist thinking end? There is no free lunch, only in robbing the productive to take for themselves, ostensi-bly, to give to the poor and "the children."

The poor are heavily subsidized to stay poor and not go to work anyway. Tax incentives giving them refunds when they had paid no taxes, redistributing incomes only made them more dependent on their politicians. Confused social programming has made California a haven for the illegal immigrants and a great place for non-citizens and those residing abroad, retired and on welfare programs of various types take SS benefits with them. Discussing these programs can be someone else's book.

It will take a few years for refineries to ready their production to any new standard, which has not been forthcoming. Besides, the refineries want to charge nearly 15% more for the same amount of energy and they were trying to sandbag the regulators in Sacramento to approve of the charges.

This oil marketing and refining was becoming a virtual monopoly in California what with all the merging and bureaucratic decisions being made for the industry. Without building a new refinery in over ten years, in late June 2001, the price of gasoline dropped sharply by 10%. So how long can they keep prices bouncing off the ceiling? They must pay the price now with the lowered revenues at retail prices around a dollar a gallon, half what they were charging at the peak in the same year. Astounding, is it not?

Do you have any questions for your elected officials, the President, environmentalists, your service station, your broker? How could such things be allowed to happen in this well-regulated economy, managed by monopoly, either in the state or in private companies? The mere threat of competition scares the oil marketers.

The point is that when the trend changes, marketers and govern-ment regulators try to keep prices more stable, especially on the high side. Failing to do so, the market cavitates and prices collapse, slower than they are allowed to rise for there is no place to store excess inventories. They have developed short lead-time from manufacture to delivery into vehicles.

Refinery shutdowns are undesirable because a whole range of product is lost creating spot shortages. It is not easy to shut down a refinery and likewise it is difficult to reopen one. On reopening, all the ecologists want to add new restrictions to update their agenda. The real question then appears: If they cannot control the demand cycle, then they do not have control of the production cycle. Who does control the demand?

That is the natural cycle of consumers quite logically, the cycles that track the trend 18, 20 and 37-year major cycles, the natural forces that govern man. So, now you know the secret oh voters of America, politicians in high places, bureaucrats with agenda and managers of industry! Perform your little acts as you were taught in trade schools, university of hard knocks and universities of great prestige and endowments, then, complain to government agencies, Congress and the President to gain help when your business skills fail you and nature takes over anyway.

It is no wonder the politicians were playing the game in California with them for the oil industry was buying elections with contributions, favors almost by the hour. They do it in most states and international supply sources. Everyone likes a nice bribe now and then to keep up the morale of the bureaucratic leaders and to balance their personal budgets.

In America, our people and corporations are not permitted to bribe a foreign government's agencies or personnel, but the Federal Government can. It has reserved bribery of foreign officials and leaders for itself. No wonder we get along with certain countries, and others who don't get as much in bribes complain and call us names. They teach their little kids to hate us because they aren't getting their share of the loot as compared to another potentate or nation.

Until the next election in 2002 in the State of California, there is likely to be little change, but the jabbering of political candidates who fill the airwaves. The evidence is that they have done nothing in the past 12 months except to compound the natural problems. That is another story and not pertinent to this forecast.

30

Gerrymandering Will End the Liberal

Gerrymandering will end the liberal control (of legislatures nation-wide.)

One of the reasons for the vicious electioneering of the 2000-year election was to control voting districts change along party lines for the next group of politician's elections. There was an attempt to shift power from declining rural and small state population centers into the growing cities and states. This would overcome the need to dispose of the Electoral College putting control over the party into the Big City machines.

The eight largest cities try to control the vote nationally, since they have more welfare/vote buying/minority programs still in place among non-English speaking, the poor and union groups.

Liberals want to expand the dependency, too. Some regions of major cities have even greater budgets for SS benefits and health care programs than other parts of the city. Country and county rural areas are being short changed nearly 50% in the Medicare funding of HMO's. They have had years to correct the laws, but they won't because the liberal Congress is comfortable with the vote buying results they legislated. When the Congress is more conservatively organized, you will see more balancing of programs. This may take as long as a decade to begin to occur.

Across the nation the independent business operators, farmers, transportation services, medical and myriad of fiercely independent people follow these changes and support the Electoral College vote given by the Constitution. The writers of the Constitution compromised with the rural states to protect them from the tyranny of large populations in the larger cities.

Voter control by the larger cities could easily impose their values on the rest of the nation. This was one of the reasons the founding fathers of the states demanded the balancing of control over New York, Philadelphia, Boston and other developing cities while the independent people moved westward.

To invalidate the Electoral College with changes by voting blocks of special interest groups would invalidate the Constitution, hence, the rebalancing of elected representatives and the inclusion of new residents is essential for fair elections.

During the coming 2002 and 2004 election years the political party in power will attempt, within recent court restrictions, to mount a plan to maintain control over their state political territory.

Gerrymandering was a practice in the last century, initiated by Elbridge Gerry of Massachusetts in 1812, wherein lines were drawn almost by the city block to prevent the opposing party from gaining power while protecting their own voter in neighborhood blocks. The lines rambled wildly over the terrain becoming a scandal of illogical voting patterns.

It is over in many states now, but it can be a powerful tool in tighter areas of political interest. New laws limit the amount of peculiar line drawing for political control and may well make the practice a minor technique in the future.

While the liberals will lose power in this decade, other parties and ideas may well appear to replace them and challenge many of the Republican proposals, moderating the changes normally expected.

31

Governor Gray Davis, California

Governor Gray Davis will never be Governor again nor become President!

He has the big war chest to launch the grand campaign. He has the support of Senators Boxer and Feinstein. They helped him get the votes in 2000 when he was on the ropes for his next turn in office.

The energy crisis and the mal-management of solutions blown over the airways almost daily for the solution that began in 1996 with the incomplete de-regulation, showed his shallow and inept management ability. The utilities and unions had bought and paid for much of his election in year 2000 so that he would not interfere with their plan for milking the public electrical and gas users.

He can never again gain political ascendancy in California even though he has amassed one of the greatest political funds for a run for the Presidency in the coming few years. His record from the days when he was Jerry Brown's Chief of Staff many years ago and Brown now manages as Mayor of Oakland is definitely socialist and liberal. He is quoted by the liberal media and network TV from time to time, if you do not remember Brown. He is the son of Pat Brown, governor of California before Ronald Reagan took him out by a landslide.

32

Hoof & Mouth Disease, a Threat

If this destructive disease, as spread by the wind and by touch, is discovered within the U.S. the price of beef, hogs and lamb will rise dramatically, or else most of us will become vegetarians. This could become a grave ingredient for the increase in food inflation.

A severe decline in beef product use shows a fall off in Europe of 85%, in Spain 70%. Animal fat products like cosmetics and facial creams can carry the disease. Humans are not subject to the disease as are cattle, sheep and other farm animals, but can cause ugly effects unwittingly delivered by cosmetics.

Andrews believes the Agriculture Dept will keep it under control but inflation is another subject. Let us watch and track.

33

Hoof & Mouth Disease Discovery

In Thailand, veterinarians have developed an antidote for the disease and have been successful in their country thereby avoiding the killing of flocks and herds. One wonders, after the turn of the WTC towers into rubble whether this is part of the scheme to destroy the United States and Capitalism by disease and pestilence.

The disease was last seen in 1929 in the United States. This strange repetition that once occurred with the speculation in the stock markets, like in the '29 era is repeating. Is it the heat of the climate at this time that activates the pestilence, or are they similar cycles? What's the connection? What condition is this replicating? Suddenly it is endemic in Europe and England. This is a strange phenomenon, and was also found in western Canada infrequently in the early 50's. This suggests a recurring period of about 70 years and is suspected as being a cause from the higher than average temperatures found then and now. It is spread mostly by the wind and contact. Chlorine and vinegar solutions seem to kill the virus. Should the animals survive starvation, most mature animals would recover in about six weeks.

But Mad Cow disease is something that was a pure hygienic failure of the health authorities in Europe. Imagine feeding livestock (born to live on grasses) the bones and body remains of their fellow herd grass eaters. Somehow, the connection is in the feed line, not in the breeding lines of the animals. We have goofed again. It is this way that society learns, perhaps slowly.

34

Housing, Homes and Construction

No subject is closer to the heart of an economist, banker, politician, or contractor than mortgage and construction lending. With continued population increases the need for housing will remain the dominant industry in this nation. Remodeling and updating houses remains a major activity.

Where and when populations do stagnate and perhaps begin to decline, no construction industry can long remain profitable in the way we see home building today, for it would become a shrinking society and feeding on itself as a bear market compresses. Remodeling has the only potential for the trade unions and contractors.

Suburbs have become the preferred place to live as long as the commute to the job was reasonable. Retirement out of the big city with cash from home sales has built the rural atmosphere into small cities. No need to go to the big city to work. It was a dream fulfilled for many. Something is happening though that takes the joy out of home ownership today.

There is this condition developing in Southern California, the Bay area cities, probably noticed in the northwest too, Texas, Illinois and upstate New York, all of which had become dependant on cheap energy.

That time has passed. Consequently, many of the big energy users will build new plants out of state in Nevada, Texas, Mexico and other energy-friendly sites and take their employees along.

What about the big influx of people California usually has? People go where there are jobs or better jobs and living is good, retire where they can afford it with their savings. Illegal immigrants go where they can get better pay and good living without having to wait in line for legal papers. The open border says to them "Come on in!"

"We'll give your children free and easy citizenship, free hospitals, free educations, free civil rights and you can keep your dual Mexican citizenship, and you can run back home as often as you wish without fear of losing your green card. You can buy homes, a car, clothes, unemployment insurance, and retirement benefits and get free food at the shelter, if you lose your job."

In addition, the Mexican agenda is to take back California after their defeat in the days of California's gold rush. They want the territory back, infrastructure and all. This is one reason they are piling over the border to claim jurisdiction again. War? Maybe!

Combine this with the new Presidente Vicente Fox de Mexico and you get the formula for change. How many of the illegal Latinos are likely to go back to help the president rebuild the Mexican industrial base with experienced and trained people with dual citizenship? Probably few, considering the prosperity differences of the two countries and cultures.

Let's put another factor into the pot. Suppose there were fewer jobs for these non-citizens due to a great world economic slowdown and population decline. Then, because of the recessive nature of the economy, welfare programs, free schooling, hospital care and other elements now attracting South Americans could become unavailable.

How many would likely return to their homelands? Many would drift southward to take up their old lifestyles. The young would likely remain for they were born and bred here. They may not speak English, but who cares anyhow. It's an open border. They have no loyalty to America for it is their freebie.

Maybe this is the first opportunity we can get to reseal the border until we can get an agreement among our political elected and think-tanks that makes sense instead of political correctness.

All this adds up to a serious slowdown in demand for new and old houses and in central cities in deteriorating slum landlord neighborhoods. Vacancies rise, no one wants to maintain the home, uninsured and the homeless take over the projects. Slums expand into neater neighborhoods causing more flight to suburbs.

That shifts the inflow to outgo and it is a heck of a lot cheaper to live in the rural Mexican country, even with the welfare programs found in our southwest than in the old U.S. of A with its minimums and heavy taxes. The exodus continues draining cheap labor southward.

Those homes in Southern California now occupied by Spanish speaking families, and groups living within, may become vacant. The occupant density will decrease, regardless. Sales Tax revenues will decrease. Schools will have fewer bilingual students. Industry will hire fewer workers, etc.

Now comes the kicker! Home re-sales will slow while new construction will shrink along with automobile and traffic problems. Minority labor will become a drag on the market and some new tract construction, which may not be approved by lenders. Even though the banks and S & L's may have adequate funds, the risk may be too high for developers. Lower levels of construction is a characteristic of the 18 and 37-year cycle lows, plus lag times for permits, financing, plans.

Vacancies could rise and repossessions could be expected to surge for those whose cash-to-carry resources are limited. Until recently, Latino immigrants had not been buying homes because they were afraid of economic declines when they might become out of work. They have been buying in recent years, ownership being promoted by the Latino agencies.

Loan forfeitures will absorb a good amount of the cash reserves for banks buying back loans, and Fannie Mae may raise the interest rates again.

Now, that doesn't make sense—or does it? Not unless it is near the 2007-8 major cycle housing lows. Now, do you begin to comprehend that until the cycle bottoms out, all the intermediate shifting rates does little to announce the major turning point.

Alan Greenspan Chairman of the FRB is in a tight spot trying to cover the hot roof like cats sometimes do. Similarly, cities like Latino-rich Fresno, Southern California and suburbia Sacramento will find vacancy factors rising. Better income people have already moved to suburbia.

Mortgage Bankers Association is suggesting that long-term mortgage rates are still headed downward. Why have rates fallen against the economic decline when they usually rise? We'll have to wait and see what develops to correct this condition. Perhaps we have not finished the interest rate cycle that peaked in 1982. If it is in that 20-year bracket with the down leg still moving lower, we may not bottom until summer 2002. The next peak of interest rates would project to be in the 2022 time zone. That would drive down bonds and real estate prices, would it not?

During recessive periods, these interest rates for mortgage loans have usually gone up and points are added because of sudden demand for new or to refinance existing loans. We should do some new research in this area over the next few years.

Many Latinos have gone to Seattle, Vancouver, Portland, Chicago, Detroit, New York, Miami and most of Florida. With lower demand for their labor, more cities than just in California will be affected.

Farm labor may not be as involved in the exodus, but many of the major cities will take a hit. Industrial declines into the Crash into 2008 will continue until inventories are depleted and demand reorders reappear in industry, thereby keeping employment lower than is to be expected in most years.

The opportunity to correct many of our border and legal problems will prevail into the 2010 period regardless of who is elected to the Presidency before then.

The political fall-out of this recession period will be far greater than 90% of the economists of the world are now predicting. We were invulnerable, just like with the 1929 thinking. Today, much of the attitude of those days found in 1929 still prevail in this economy, in spite of the next short-term cycle rally now appearing in spring 2002 and expected to continue through the year 2002.

35

Leadership Shifts Dominate, Trends Change

When George W. Bush was finally certified as the President, the liberal legislators, news media, TV, and newspapers were belligerent and demonstrated this in their copy. The review of the votes by Miami newspapers and USA Today gave even greater numbers of votes to Bush, and still they used the Gore standard for counting. They announced Bush the winner in early April 2001. Still, large factions of the Democratic (liberal side) of the Party insists that Al Gore was elected and Joe Lieberman is unofficial VP. What crass! Credit should be given to Al Gore in a speech in September when he said "Bush is my president and I support him."

After the first year of the Bush Administration, it was discerned that he had charmed them, brought them to his side, and turned many of the venomous liberal ideas and legislators into supporters for his programs. He was open and honest, never wavering, once he set his goals. A few hard liners hope to upset the cart before the 2002 election. At year-end 2001, Tom Daschle began his campaign by blocking as many programs and judicial appointments as he could to make Bush look incompetent and to hamstring his programs.

California is gone from the Democratic Party block now, with the energy crisis mismanagement by Gray Davis and his appointees. Californians will pay the price for many years to come for his sabotage of the energy industry. His public career is likely over.

36

Liberal Wing of Democratic Party

It was top heavy with welfare and vote-buying programs in order to control their power base. The public is turning against them as it sees the shams of their boondoggles. Publicity and publicizing, the games being played on the voters with energy issues, is educating the voter.

The Democratic Party, conservative wing, will remain and reorganize gradually moving the liberals out of positions of authority. The sooner the better, if the party is to survive the pressures of coming changes.

What of the liberal's power base? It is likely, instead of playing games with the Democratic leaders, they will go with the more obvious—Socialist/Communist Party of America. They vote that way anyway and the public is noticing their bias. So why not make the big move before it's too late? Then again, is socialism on its last legs?

37

Line Budgeting—Integrity in Government

There is a new way of accounting in the public domain. Since 1999, a Goals and Performance Measures study has shifted from spending the tax money, as a planning process, to the "results" oriented plan. San Luis Obispo County (CA) has been proud to introduce this concept in all areas as the SEA (Service, Efforts and Accomplishments) report is an attempt to measure the results of its administrative organizations to become more effective and to improve communications with the public.

It's a report card on how well the agency and the County are aimed at more than just counting number of calls or service provided. Rather, "we are cutting out the waste and meaningless reports and getting better ambulance, fire, police, community service for the dollar costs."

It is so easy for bureaucrats to lengthen and compound the administrative procedures so they don't need to work as hard. Idleness seems preferred to work when the incentives to do better are missing. Measures of output in terms of quality are needed in every political center.

Every legislative program should have a sunset clause for it to be reviewed for need, at least.

In our political thinking, that is why we need to clean the house of the laggards and dullards who get little done. They do like that paycheck on Friday, regular and without having to be too smart. That is why budget cuts will prevail into the end of the decade until the tax base gets healthier with improving business and fewer deadheads. Bureaucrats can outwait the elected officers and then resume their stodgy self-serving ways.

Nature gave us these cyclical recessions like economic cycles so that the non-productive personnel in the organization or group can be recycled to some other line of work. Why haven't our elected leaders moved when the opportunity appeared?

Will this procedure reach the State Legislatures and be practiced as a cost-cutting measure? Will it reach the Feds? Don't you think we are deep enough into the hog rut where agencies just fill the trough with food and employees take it and stuff themselves? Cut off the excess food, calculate what a hog needs and save the balance for other needs or bad economic days.

They complain they are underpaid. Nonsense, they are overpaid and fat bureaucrats. Clean the sheds protecting these special interest agencies and all the excess bureaucracy now. Once the surplus is gone, a tax increase will become the official legislature talk again. The surplus is gone already and "we got no cut in our taxes in California," Bob said. This is leading us into the California Crash of 2008.

Since 51% of the boomers in Washington DC jobs are now eligible for retirement, this would be a good time to not fill vacancies, cut the funding to what is needed in these times. Let the bureaucracy shrink steadily as retirees are allowed to go back to the village and their own home town.

38

Mad Cow Disease and Man

What more would you have them do than keep trying to correct errors from mixing animal protein with grain feed to cut costs? This was a big surprise a few years ago when the reports from England indicated this had been a practice for years. Then the big surprise was the same in Europe and here in the states. There have been a lot of poor food preparation practices here and abroad that just got sloppier and deliberately used to cut costs and dispose of problems.

Perhaps it was just such liberal veterinary and animal husbandry health practices without supporting tests and data that is now causing the conservative thinking concept to take over in politics and in public attitudes. The threat will hang around man for many years. Because it is a disease it takes time to appear in another animal or person; it may take years before an epidemic appears.

Mad Cow Disease reaches out for man

Most assuredly it will become a best killer of man in future years. With all those hamburgers and beef products hustled by the fast food industry that did carry the virus, it is unlikely we will escape. Whether the cause of the mind destroying disease made famous by President Reagan, Alzheimer's will be found to have been a contributor from eating beef, or not. Proving the real cause is possibly the only answer. We will just have to wait until evidence can be traced. The blending of ground beef with sick animal and diseased animals is normal practice.

Should not the FDA (Food & Drug Administration) tighten standards, or like every other incident, do nothing and let things return to normal. Don't rock the political campaigns by not getting contributions from the food suppliers who practice unsafe food preparation.

One of the diagnostic problems facing the medical profession is that once surgical tools touch a Mad Cow specimen during an autopsy, that instrument may not be used again. There has been no way found to sterilize tools and facilities where the animal is dissected. Surgeons refuse to operate on Mad Cow disease cadavers. The risk of contact is too great. When and how research can be done is as yet unknown. Alzheimer patients only get autopsies. We have much to learn.

Switzerland has developed an antibiotic serum injection for cattle. Hopefully, it will also work on humans.

Now we hear that the deer, elk wolf, fox, and lesser animal populations have taken the disease.

It is conjecture, but it looks like the population explosion we have been hearing about is about to be eclipsed by shortened life-spans as well as the shrinking birth rates in most developed countries the same as found in oceans and on farms.

39

Media Excesses, Without Facts

Sloppy reporting has become the norm in the past decade, if not for several decades of journalistic values. Most distressing is the tendency of various networks to "pile-on" with a news story and beat it to death, or until another big story blows it off the daily news.

One of the problems has been the AP (Associated Press) as the press news source for the network owners, has become a monologue. UP (United Press) has similar habits. Now one group of reporters sifts the news viewed through their agenda screen-driven values, as they were brought up, and learned in journalism schools. Then they distribute their version to the four major networks. The networks save money that way. Besides, they own AP.

We hope this sole provider will be replaced with more independent competition. That's why the reporter stories read and sound the same all day long and as repeated by different networks. Fox tried to be objective with their reporting. Something happened! All five news networks sound an awful lot like each other, news and sequence of stories.

Lazy news anchors (readers) with long-term contracts have been repeating each story live, and amazingly, they do the same story nearly verbatim off the AP printer and onto the screen in sequences that repeat almost exactly in time frames with Peter Jennings, Tom Brokaw and Dan Rather. Viewers are able to click each channel and not miss a word in the reports. It was the same on every channel. And, for that they get paid millions from advertisers who expect us to buy their products to pay for this lethargy? There is a major shift of influence developing that reporters are not worth the cost of their services.

CNN also continues to report repeating stories too, but has been changing anchors recently. It has created newsworthy stories that proved more like propaganda, than unbiased reporting.

The rumor is they wanted to hire Rush Limbaugh, the conservative talk show host because he has a conservative following of millions. Rush didn't take the bait or money. He lost his hearing in three months and now relies on technical tools to interpret voice and sounds. With surgery he has recovered 80% of his hearing. They are attempting to look balanced, but is it too late?

Advertising revenues continue to falter having dropped precipitously in the past two years for the network TV stations. It's a scramble to keep the balance sheet looking ok. The reprieve in 2002-03 with recovery will help, but if things do not increase profits during that time, the following market panic will break a few of the networks, and maybe all three will reorganize.

Then the Fox network with Bill O'Riley leading the charge against many news stories and planted propaganda and other news reporters, did more in depth reporting and began to drive the liberal view off the screen, challenged authority after authority who were putting out the spin from the liberal encampment. Fox became #1 in spring 2001. Wow, that hurts the other networks. Will Fox moderate?

It is small wonder the major TV network and cable channels started reporting lower viewer numbers and the financial panic began to show. Advertising dollars started to disappear from the old-line shows and some of it started to go to Fox's programming.

Andrews predicts there will be new anchors in all four old-line channels (already showing on CNN with Ted Turner's firing) within the next two years. Finally, in 2007-8 stability may begin to return to programming and anchors.

A review of news-gathering practices will open up the opportunities for a variety of new opinions. In a sense, the AP monopoly is broken already and the advertisers are moving over to the radio media with the greatest integrity and coverage.

The high prices paid for sport TV spots may have peaked. If recent events are any judge, then there is a slowing in budgeting for the big events and probably an equal decline in local and regular national sport activity. From some university comments, there seems to be some cutting back on University level football funding. We'll have to wait and see the unfolding of recessive activity. Remember the baseball team strike? Fans returned!

The TV shows are due for major overhaul. XFL turning in a dismal record on NBC and finally shutting down suggests a decline in sports programming and big salaries to players. Higher ticket prices are making the games prohibitive, unless you have a corporate sponsor. Filling the seats looks to be a problem just appearing. Perhaps they will start to give away free team coffee cups to get the seats filled.

It used to be the filling stations giving away glasses, theatres giving away sets of china to winners of the bingo crowds. Those were depression years, some of you will remember.

It is reported that female fans have dominated the past 40-50 years coming into sports regularly. They are now leveling off. Does this mean ticket prices are too high or that the fans are interested in other things, at the moment?

Radio has been taking over the news with higher numbers of listeners and commentary that much of the TV network had controlled for years. Movies have shrunk in quality and with higher ticket prices. Cost cutting continues. Where else can a couple of teenagers go to get their giggles and test their hormones? They are maturing so early now, as opposed to 100 years ago.

Radio night and day is getting more listeners and there are few liberal anchors left. "Jimbo," Jim Bohannon, one of the many, keeps losing audience while there are increasing numbers of other anchor talk show hosts who are conservative and getting more advertising budget. Jimbo replaced Larry King, and now has an anchor show on CNN.

East coast, particularly in the northeastern states, has more liberal hosts and followers and has an adequate supply of their radio hosts allowing liberal discussions. The new hosts are more conservative. National radio shows are more conservative than local jockeys.

There used to be the commute talk show and hosts with helicopter interruptions. Many still remain, but the off-peak hour trip-to-work listener is taking on the leadership and going for conservative talk show hosts using cellular phones often.

The author has noticed that his TV viewing time has been cut in half. He reads more, listens to talk radio more and corresponds more. How many out there notice that they are doing alternate activity?

As for the movies, they seem to have few or original ideas and redeemable thoughts and the high priced tickets aren't worth the effort. It seems that younger singles and dating couples prefer the movies. Look for renewed efforts to spark the movie houses. It is unfortunate, but foreign movie viewers judge the American society by the movies they view, in English or dubbed. We have a reputation that is not always defined by a proud tourist.

So where do we go from here? More backyard barbecues, poker and card games? Travel was getting killed with high fuel costs and high hotel/motel prices in the heavens with surcharges. Ever since bin Laden crashed at least two airliners full of fuel into the WTC and another one into the Pentagon building, then one that was crashed into Pennsylvanian soil by doomed passengers, traffic has dropped. Fuel costs collapsed since the closing of airports that day, and continue to remain in excess supply. People are not traveling like they were prior to the peak of the economy in summer 2000.

Cruising is finding competition as new ships are launched. There has to be something that is worth the effort to share in the evening and not get reruns and propaganda thrown in our faces on television. Perhaps, during this recessive period into *year ought eight*, entertainment designers can come forward with something that is different and more wholesome to the listeners and viewers. How about a new twist to the same old thing? Books may be the sole answer to this problem. If the book monopoly begins to entertain new writers and publish a few more new authors may have best selling books instead of the same old guys and gals being designated for the books the publisher wants to see on the shelf.

Children TV programming has reached such a repetitive stage that many kids are turning off—it's old stuff to them. Still each new generation is subject to the old beat-'em-up and kill 'em dead fare that has been getting worse every year. Producers keep trying with new serials, but few make two seasons. Kids still don't realize that once dead, forever dead, not just in movies, but in real life.

Hula hoops™ still comes out for every new generation like the skateboard and bicycle manufacturers. Trying to find something new to get the kid's attention seems to be the reason. Many viewers are cutting the TV connection and insisting the kids study or read instead.

Saturation is reaching the cable networks as consolidation continues.

Where do you suppose the kids get the ideas about life, except from observing their parents and neighbors? It's the boobtoob! When parents begin to demonstrate their values, the kids will pick it up, imitate them, but not while they are watching TV. Some may be outside throwing rocks down the street at other gangs, if they don't have guns.

The violence on TV and in movies has been training our kids to act out their anger and frustration, when derived from lack of parental discipline, to drug-induced activity for overactive kids. Is it any wonder shootings occur on campuses? In frustration and in anger against not being disciplined to do the right thing has made kids feeling unloved. They respond well to early discipline and direction when given before reaching their terrible teens.

Andrews thinks this will be changing now that the excesses of the 90's seem to have passed while the heat of the climate extremes is projected to become more moderate in coming years. Kids will likely get more family discipline in relationships and more approval with less violent games on video and "Pacman™" type of gamesmanship with blood flying and guns blasting the other guy.

40

Minimum Wage is Inflationary

Sounds like a "no brainer" idea. But the name of the game is to get something for nothing and politicians like to claim they are supporting the poor so the poor will vote for them at election time. Landlords tend to raise rents by about the same amount of the monthly net increase in tenant incomes each year. So, how can renters benefit? So, how do we legislate morality and integrity?

Subsidies are inflationary as are higher taxes, increased health costs, higher energy prices, restraints on buildings, court legislature acts, congressional pay raises, state block pay raises, etc.

41

National Energy Policy Versus OPEC

Is OPEC a monopoly? Since OPEC (Organization of Petroleum Exporting Countries) is an admitted oligopoly, or near monopoly, it cannot be prosecuted as a domestic oil company. It could be when favoring limiting production, withholding supplies and giving egregious price raises. Since the member countries control the major supplies of petroleum they can dictate the terms to oil dependant countries, like U.S. with 60% of needs imported.

The environmentalists have been using oil controls to gain their socialist ends keeping oil fields and refining activity to a minimum. We are getting more dependent on oil than ever!

Our ecological socialists have prevented drilling, production, refining and marketing wherever possible adding to the costs of and shrinking the domestic supply.

None will take responsibility for the chaos caused by the California energy crisis, nor for the impending national oil crisis. If they were so competent in denying the drilling and marketing, why should ecologists not want to stand proud and responsible for keeping the supply so low that populations must crowd into the larger cities in desperation, cut back on travel and use of machinery to manufacture product or electrical energy?

Now the crunch hit California hard. Where are the proud ecologists and environmentalists? Did this crunch move into the other states steadily?

Strangely, since the peak of retail oil prices in April 2001 at near $2.00 gallon, oil prices have been collapsing and by end of 2001 prices were below $1.00 in Los Angeles and other major cities. How could this happen? Industry and commercial layoffs and recession demand for consumer products suddenly declined. But that bunch of layoffs was in the last half of the year. The World Trade Center disaster and recession came after the declines in employment levels began.

Often, with such WTC disasters, the following few days tell the story. If the markets continue to decline for weeks or months, a severe depression will follow, but if within the following week the up-trend market rally resumes, the worst is over. Presidents have heart attacks and offer buying opportunities to alert unemotional investors.

The experts warned that gasoline might hit $3.00 a gallon in the summer of 2001, in just a few months. Remember the experts who, when gold hit $825 oz. that it would hit $1000 within just a few months. It collapsed just like oil did recently.

Do you remember the rule mentioned earlier about elections, etc.? This is a reminder, when the experts and over 67% or plurality of people think similarly and with the press reiterating the story in headlines, the end of the move is near. It used to be that when the newspapers had a big story on the "gas war," the end came before sunup the next day with the price back to normal.

It may be the top or the bottom of a trend. Now that suggests a cycle factor is involved, not supply or demand alone, although demand precedes increasing supplies pushing the need before the supply begins to meet the demand. Prices begin to rise for other reasons as consumption use and needs rise. This is the time when oil, drilling and marketing stocks signal a buy point first among oil services. At the same time, overzealous traders and investors reach an extreme, then, the reversal is near.

It all began in the 60's with Rachel Carson's book, *Silent Spring* wherein she outlined the death of birds, coral and weak egg shells of species causing a fall in their reproduction rate. The use of herbicides was polluting the lands, reservoirs, rivers, lakes, seas and oceans of the world.

Mankind was being threatened with the side effects of these man-made pesticides and drugs. We still make them but with more understanding of their long-term implications and side effects. This revised chemical composition has reduced the risk greatly. However, have we gone over the edge into over-kill? That will be determined by history as society struggles to rebalance progress versus environmentalism in society.

There has been great talk (spin) of shortfalls in production as well as supply in the ground since oil wells were invented a century ago. There are greater proven reserves today than ever in the history of oil exploration. Still, we know that one day it will become more difficult to find, and the oil price will become well above the common man's ability to pay. This brings us to the alternate energy, which will be covered later.

Late in the 19th Century, John D. Rockefeller had amassed control of the oil industry in a vertical integration from wellhead to gasoline pump. The demand was modest since there were few autos on the non-existent highways. He forced mergers to be made with him by colluding with the railroads to charge other oil shippers a very high price for the oil while he was given kickbacks on their shipments. As various wildcatters found no market left to them they were forced to sell to Rockefeller's companies.

Of course, he was making a lot of money by under-pricing other suppliers with his own low freight charge with his oil competitors paying a steeper shipping charge.

Justice Department found him guilty of anti-trust and broke up his industry monopoly. It is no longer legal to do many things the way he did to gain the monopoly. Gasoline made the motor vehicle possible and highway systems brought the nation together. We need this network to serve all states of North America.

Route 66 was the main east to west road even though it was little more than a series of logs over sand in some desert areas, mud holes in others, river fords and narrow bridges. But, technology brought us to where we have TV, radio, cell phones, off-road capability, campers, big vans and truckers with dual and triple trailers, as big as boxcars of the old days, roaming the twin concrete ribbons, all-weather concrete roads from city to city with cargo for all. This road building of interstate highways began during President Eisenhower's term in office after WW II.

Airlines came and speeded up the travel to major destinations. Now we are coming into a new form of transport! What is it? We'll have to wait and see what the industry devises.

Internet has reduced the need for considerable travel. Voice and video added to the computer will alter much travel need and increase conferencing calls. Doing business face-to-face is again possible on the keyboard. By 2008, when the Crash is due, most people will be able to talk to each other over computer screens. Travel will be for fun and experience, but not so much for business.

There is always someone in the industry trying to gain a control over some territory or level of production to manipulate prices to make outlandish profits. Be on guard. Airlines are merging to accomplish the same effects, as has the oil business, radio, TV, cable TV, software, water services, long distance telephone and data carriers, power sources and merchandisers all attempt to gain a semi-monopoly or oligopoly in some form. Carving out a niche is one thing but killing off the competitors is bad. Sometimes it is inevitable that the competition is underfunded or technologically inferior to the leading company.

Free markets and free enterprise is a good slogan to keep government at bay from prosecuting them, but when someone else does the same thing, they yell for government lawyers to harass them, the other guys are cutting into their territory.

This means only one thing: The source of motive power and electrical energy must be from cold fusion or conversion of seawater to hydrogen for newly designed auto vehicle and independent power plants for home and industry. Petroleum will then become a chemical and lubricant much like anthracite coal had become a chemical element from the Allegheny coal-mines. It is no longer mined as fuel in most areas where it exists. Andrews projects working energy generator models in larger cities by 2008 supplanting some power lines.

42

New Age is Coming, Now

Election reversals signal the new age is coming! In Israel, Barak got 40.5% Sharon 59.5% of votes in February 6, 2001 election, a confirming turn of the times. In Canada, we now have a conservative Premier.

Like Vicente Fox in Mexico, the conservatives are arriving. France, typically, elected a new socialist leader this year. Japanese leader was replaced in April 2001 as their economy was collapsing much as ours was under William Jefferson Clinton when he left office to find his legacy.

Tony Blair in England managed to be reelected as Prime Minister. When he is defeated and replaced with a conservative Prime Minister we will know the change is nearly complete. He called off the May 2001 election due to pressing matters concerning the Hoof and Mouth Disease problem. But he still has a good following in his battle to stay clear of the EU and their new currency.

Japanese markets collapsed into '89 cycle lows. Interest rate is ½% today and is likely to go almost to zero in their attempt to rejuvenate their industrial base. This is comparable to the U.S. crash in '29 when margin rates were low at 10% and almost anything qualified for a loan to invest in the market.

The Crash of '29 was exacerbated by the margin calls going out to borrowers with few assets and practically no cash, hence portfolios were sold out as the market fell. Raising import duties with the Smoot-Hawley Tariff, cut business sharply.

Today, we have mutual funds where much of the bad investing practice has been eliminated. This cushions the market fall and is the reason why it is hard to calculate support and resistance price levels. Fundamental analysts believe this is the way the market works. In reality, it is the reverse. The cycle brings investors into a frame of mind that allows opportunity and greed to appear. After the economy begins to resurrect, earnings reappear in about two quarters. This is mentioned in other sectors of the book, also. Therefore, cycles dominate the moves, fundamentals follow! But, even the fund managers got complacent and let Enron happen, along with Kmart, Global Crossing and many Internet companies.

Pessimism still abounds in the markets

Layoffs are building in spite of federal statistics. How can the Bureau of Labor Statistics continue to put out misleading, delayed employment numbers with almost daily cutbacks and layoffs being reported? After benefits are ended, the unemployed are no longer counted and the numbers out of work fall. There will be many changes in Washington by 2008 giving us more accurate numbers on the economy, and how much money is really being spent to improve quality of labor.

As the new year 2002 begins, the unemployment level reached 5.8% the highest in six years and rising sharply. Nixon got tossed out when unemployment reached over 7% after his peak of popularity in his second term election. Politicians love to expound on such statistics to rip their opposition. The depression has nothing to do with politics in the U.S. or as in Argentina for their excesses in borrowing from the World Bank to fund increased industrial potential. Many nations did the same thing in the roaring twenties, never paying off the bonds, notes and obligations that made the Great Depression so terrible. The same happened to Japan and they are paying the price in this second 18-year cycle.

There are other nations in the world which will pay the price also. Coming to mind as big spenders are the oil producing nations. They have been living very prosperously on high oil prices since the early 80's as they built OPEC. Now that oil prices are falling, in spite of reduced production, their obligations for construction and other spending will bring them to heel. The Saudi's have given the Islam Mosque centers funds for supporting their Islam community to keep unrest among the Koran following peoples from exploding in their front yards. Americans will have to deal with this inroad into our culture. Let us hope it is manageable. Their Mosques are the fastest growing religious body in America. Why are the Saudis exporting Islam?

43

Presidential Candidates

Presidential Candidates: Who are likely for 2004?

The first mentioned is Senator Hillary Clinton (who denies any interest), then another socialist Al Gore, the "has been" Vice-President (who will try again), socialist Senator Joe Lieberman, VP candidate and still a Senator who wants to run again and is making speeches to build a base; liberal Senator John Kerry of Massachusetts has announced it as his goal. Then, liberal Delaware Senator Joseph Biden, liberal Governor Gray Davis of California (he hungers for it but has become the laughing butt of jokes with his inept handling of the energy crisis et al in 2000), liberal Senator Diane Feinstein from San Francisco and ex-Councilwoman with (apologetic) ties to China and her SF Chinese constituency. (Many of the newly arrived Chinese and recent citizens supported the Chinese propaganda line when our surveillance plane was forced down on Hainan Island. In May 2001 Reverend Al Sharpton threw his hat into the ring for President, and there are others who have dreams of great power. Even former President Bill Clinton may try again; after all there is a break in continuity here. First they must all get funding and a constituency, register in every state as a candidate and get out the vote. With so many candidates, the party is badly fractured leaving little funding to promote a single stronger leader.

After Clinton and a few others in history who got elected without having any credentials and little integrity, why not try? What was once a respected office is now politics of opportunity. Clinton acts as though he will try again in 2004 since there is no law opposing his reentry into the Administration and Hillary claims she won't run for the job.

Then the conservative Republican Senator John McCain is trying again, opposing the conservative incumbent George W. Bush and this brings up the independent, Wisconsin Governor Jessie Ventura who is currently happy. McCain is getting to be a pain in the neck and many of us feel we were misled before and after his campaign with his rhetoric.

With the June 2001 meeting of Daschle and McCain, one suspects he is up to some scheme to support liberal goals and a chance to sabotage President Bush. It will be a dirty campaign in 2002 and 2004. It is a watershed confirmation period. Andrews believes the liberal economic campaigns of the past are unworkable in this new age, new millennium and Capitalistic fight for survival in the religious Jihad of the Muslim community.

Hands down, it's probably President George W. Bush for a second term, God willing, since it is in the 20th-year syndrome.

Why do we have so many good leaders cut short in their lives? Kismet! Some say. Maybe we should consult the stars with a more open mind than we have in the past.

Another actor married into the Kennedy clan, Arnold Swartzenegger, wants to become the next governor of California, running as a Republican. He could have made it, but backed out in May 2001 after some dirt was thrown at him by an LA Times (Democratic) newspaper article. In a sense, California's politics needs a major infusion of new leaders; the older ones are from the days when the population was half at this century turn, fifty yeas ago. A huge Hispanic population struggles for control of the state. It seems too early for their Jihad, but they have the agenda anyway. As California ideas move, they lead the nation toward Washington and the changes needed to reorient the national thinking.

Now, 2008 is a different ball game. We can project 'till we tire of it all, but we'll all have to wait for the leadership to emerge. The boomer age group is sliding into retirement so it may be the next gen (eration) that will show its political prowess to lead and who will walk out onto the stage in the Crash of 2008.

Whoever it is needs to give great direction and leadership for another four or eight years and will have a hard row-to-hoe. Many of the nation's problems seem to have been unsolved and new ones have arrived recently. Looks likely to be a conservative, not an independent and certainly not a liberal democrat will be elected in 2008 in a hard recession/depression.

44

Reliable Government Data

There is evidence that the consumer may be fooled with the many indices from the Federal government. The inflation index is believed to have been adjusted by the Clinton Administration eliminating energy and food, the two major consumer items of inflation or costs, to show only that the good times are here—not the actual condition of employment and the cost of living being measured accurately. These two items are cyclical and change the cost of living indices which trigger social security and federal employee pay raises. Deception has filled the bureaucracy, which is still liberal from the many appointments in the past 70 years. The battle over judicial appointments in 2001-2 is over who will interpret the new laws and whether liberalism can survive. Andrews believes Bush appointments will tilt the legislators back to conservative interpretations. We almost got a socialist Supreme Court.

45

Educational Misadventures

Everyone does not need a college education or even a degree to be a winner. They do need to demonstrate their talents and their persistence to do a job. They need training to do a tradesman or skilled craft job. The country is awash with degree-happy people who cannot manage their own bank accounts.

What used to be frivolous social and with fringe activity in college, with easy classes leading to degrees in soft arts (often called social sciences), Colleges and Universities have created some of the most common of degrees in such areas as ecology, social philosophy, political communication, and you name it to control and qualify people for jobs. It also creates a lot of professional educators producing questionable student products. This period of experimentation is probably over now that most eastern universities are controlled by liberal, race and political diverse ideas that have no intellectual value or to serve the nation honestly.

Hard degrees in math, physics, sciences, and even music are not increasing as fast as the population is increasing. That is why we must have advanced degrees to hold an executive position, regardless of skill. These degrees are qualifiers for some professional type of occupation and justification to keep other talent from migrating into their turf.

On the low end of the educational system are many students who are discarded. They have been boxed into welfare programs. They are left out of the educational disciplines because their skills are within their hands, and ability to perceive in multiple dimensions as an artist thinks. They are the ones who may have skills in their fingers, can sculpt, create through eye and feel in art forms, photography, printing, design ideas, production and assembly skills and products not requiring great verbal and mathematical skills.

They have motor skills, which many educated and degreed people do not possess in amounts sufficient for them to maintain their homes or even do manual labor. There are many routine jobs, which need their skills. Opportunities should be provided.

Case: Longaberger, a student cast off as dumb, incapable of education, stuttered and lived in a small town in southern Ohio. He did not have a chance of being anything to the community. He liked to bake bread and made wonderful bread, sold it and built a million dollar business as Longaberger Bakery.

His grandfather liked to make basket wares and tried to sell each for one dollar. There were few takers. His son raised the price to five dollars and sold them along with his bread for breadbaskets. Both prospered. He married. His daughter took over as CEO and spoke without stuttering. A chain of bakeries covers Ohio territories in spite of major chains competing against his products.

There is room for all, if only they can be encouraged to find their niche and not be put in welfare boxes and filed in subsidized housing.

Overeducated students who have been indoctrinated in university catechism as well as federal government subsidy orientation, grant and project work are the dead bureaucracy that is weighing down much of our national creativity. As a nation, we have lost sight of the goal of education: How many creative students have been ruined with four years of indoctrination?

The goal is to make a person self-sufficient and creative in both work and thought and to be able to take additional studies to upgrade skills to meet new challenges as the economy and individual grows!

We have a degree-happy educational system. Who can get a management or government job without a degree today? One cannot get any job greater than punching a time clock without a high school diploma. That is wrong! But, the people who are leading the new ways and creating the new technology are those who see opportunity first and move to maximize their potential in spite of required degrees. Usually the educational system follows the lead of new technology and then provides courses when the school discovers what has to be taught to the next group of entrepreneurs and technicians. They may be 20 years behind the times in textbooks and course criteria. Current textbooks and curriculum seem to be preaching the fantasies of the 30's. We wonder at times if the progress made in industrial development was done in spite of the educational system. Compared to the market gains made off the lows of the 30's, the educational and economic system has developed atop a massive head and shoulders? This is a technical term that formed as a market excess over 37-40 years for the top. The shoulders may be eight to ten years on each side. The overall period reaching up to 60 years, at which point the major economic and market lows require new leaders and new philosophical bent. Our previous major low of around 1000 on the Dow in 1970 may become the index (adjusted) low of 2030.

Bill Gates, now a billionaire, dropped out of college to create computer language and applications for the new technology. Dozens of his friends gave up their class work for those higher degrees then, indulging themselves in the symbolic language of zeros and ones. They are the new millionaires/billionaires. He changed the way we do business today. We are still finding new ways for using the desktop computer. Industrial concepts will open entirely new applications, should the culture survive. Under Islam it would likely be destroyed.

Besides this group of self-directing people, we have tradesmen who have learned skills using their hands and minds to build retail merchandising chairs, new industries, creators of skills unknown by their forefathers.

The public educational system has become the indoctrination center for the nation and for the political correctness of socialist central planning thinkers.

Ever since John Dewey, the nineteenth century philosopher, introduced his brand of education, it has been accepted as the nation grew. Students, undisciplined in educational needs, illiterate, numberless, unskilled in study habits, hit the colleges in 1949-50 after WWII. Our needs have expanded until the emphasis came in for vested and retirement programs. This is the aging of society.

The Winnetka System (Illinois) of progressive education was dominant in educational planning. Kids were to be passed automatically whether they could read, write, spell, do arithmetic. It was their peer group and these poor students should not be separated just because of poor grades. These students were un-drilled in the basics. They have become the core unemployed and under qualified.

From that date forward the higher public educational system became a swamp and grade standards were lowered until they have become a laugh among the thinking population. Of course, not all students were deceived by this philosophy. Many students went to private schools, church schools or were tutored in high level teaching centers for the elite and above average minds. Many learned in spite of the system where they found themselves engaged and went on to become industry giants.

Andrews expects this educational system to be severely overhauled in the next decade to gain control again by the public. Moving the system and out of the bureaucracy and to set new tough standards will be a battle royal and many socialist teachers will resign in protest.

The key to breaking the public school monopoly is in charter schools or public choice between public and either church or private educational plans. Home schools are showing such improved learning results that if the public authorities prevent public charter funding, the home school class will grow exponentially in this next decade.

Once the monopoly of unionized catechism thinking of indoctrination in the public schools has been broken, even home schooling will cease to be the answer to the social philosophies now taught in the publicly funded schools. The schools will be free again, free again and become the greatest again as new standards are developed.

The control of our schools and universities has been taken over by these "free thinkers" to revise political and social philosophy with agendas, not for educational purposes.

We began to see it in the early 30's of the twentieth century as Keynesian Economic Theory replaced old theories. It was adapted for use by President Franklin D. Roosevelt in the Great Depression. Those who have been unable to survive in business competition are stockpiled in government jobs and subsidized agencies. Too many "make-work" jobs exist in government programs. They should be privatized programs or justified every fifth year to Congress. So many bureaus exist that have little objective purpose or social need. But they continue once a crisis problem is resolved, just in case it happens again.

Like in Russia, under Communism, these people can neither be fired nor held accountable for poor workmanship, poor attitude and low productivity.

In the universities where the author taught for many years, he noted the change and deterioration and began the search for the causes of economic events and to get a better understanding of education's purpose. This is the result of some of his research.

But the degradation of learning has continued. Until an alternative is in place, it will continue to degenerate and what is not taught well in the public sector must be given as remedial graduate work (from public schools). Minimum qualifications are needed and currently only by correcting the incomplete education can it be done. We need to get ahead of the student to modernize the system and finally graduate a student competent in basics, not just one which is passed on with his peers.

The first two years of most colleges are usually remedial for the substandard education in basics (English grammar, reading, writing, arithmetic, history) provided by passing through students and keeping grade achievement requirements low. What used to be a four-year education is now a two-year upper level specialization. Wanting to get a higher education now requires a Master's degree or Ph.D. in some specialty just to get in line for a creative line of effort and achievement.

Today, these were the kids born into the progressive education concept, which began to impact school quality during the late depression years. We are, today, reaping the harvest of this thought process. These are our seniors of today just retiring after their working years.

Their children were deeply impressed with political philosophy. Many still retreat from voting in our elections feeling they are not important and nothing will be changed anyway they vote. This attitude will change when the freebies are gone or reduced to mere tokens like gold stars on the wall.

The attempt to completely socialize our society ended with the Democratic liberal wing of their party, the defeat of Al Gore and Joseph Lieberman. Liberals admittedly they were, and among them 58 at least who are publicly avowed communists. They are found among our elected Representatives and Senators and seem to be the reason why so much proposed change is blocked and watered down to junk results.

They have been redefining the Constitution and all the laws formulated against the desire of the majority. Liberals number some 20,000,000 today and control many key bureaucratic jobs, administer many of the local social programs and non-profit organizations funding socialist behavior at taxpayer expense.

Andrews expects the non-profit organizations with their tax avoiding agencies and un-audited activities, to come under closer scrutiny than legislated so far, amid great clamor for change in the next ten years.

The non-profit organization scheme has been one of the clever ways rich people have hidden their money from taxation and have been able to pursue many un-American activity programs and indoctrination schemes in the schools by pressure of subsidy speakers' bureaus, literature, reviewing text books, etc., without any supervision by other agencies or groups.

Some claim them to be supporting anti-American activities and subversive programs. Who knows how serious this claim can be? Whether government agencies should investigate or a few good reporters, is a moot question. They will be investigated because the need is there.

Vicente Fox, newly elected President of Mexico after throwing out the progressive party domination, came to Washington and then to California. He wants some of his dual citizenship "Norte Americanos" to return to Mexico to help rebuild his country.

In addition, he wants the U.S. to educate his high school graduates who are here without benefit of U.S. citizenship. He wants to have them admitted to the California university system as state residents and pay only the 8% for community colleges to 24% four-year and graduate school rates. The foreign and international student rates are $3,900 and $14,043 annually. Also he wants the U.S. to give them scholarships and grants, etc. etc.

Does this not give great incentive to peoples around the world to come to California, Texas, Illinois, NYC, and Miami without documentation under the guise of fleeing persecution? Did we ever teach the bear where the honey was? No! She could smell it. She didn't need an education. The renegades rob the honey tree daily.

No wonder foreign nations sabotage us and try to get grants and subsidies for their countries else they might get mad and try to destroy us. Should we shake in our boots, or straighten them out by controlling the border and enforcing proper citizenship rights for the children and adults when they are without documentation.

And, we wonder why our taxes are so high and climbing.

But, this game is probably over. The trend is projected to be toward more self-directing and self-responsibility to survive and prosper. Let's move on to the next level of this society. Can we afford to regress? Never go backward! But keep a rear guard watching for an ambush.

46

Soft Money

"Soft money," or money given to the national political party to use any way it wants, is destroying integrity in this government. Soft money seems to have no audit or limitations applied as to source, integrity and application. No elected person seems interested in limiting the money. Outsiders wanting a chance to be elected are complaining—they want to get in on the easy money.

Hard money, closely monitored by law is identified with a particular candidate and must be audited. As the debate continues, so does the exposure of the large contributors by special interest groups, labor and industry and the military providers of equipment to build aircraft, radar, flat tops, subs, space stuff and stuff we know nothing about called subsidies. We should not restrain political participation.

The return to the tax-deductible contribution by 50% on the tax return for say a $1000 contribution to the party of choice may enliven the public interest to voting again. Worldwide the voter turnout is still on the decline. When they lose interest in TV sports programs, perhaps then they will take up political activity.

The press of the fourth estate is highly in favor of un-ending contributions in soft and hard (to a person) money and give lots of editorial support to unfettered funding in their respective publications. Publishers like to get the advertising revenues from the candidates.

Isn't it obvious?

They get the biggest chunk of the money for the advertisement time and space in radio, TV, cable, newspapers, newsmagazines and the printers get a good sized chunk for throwaways. Telecommunications companies enjoy another sizable piece of the action while the Postal Service just drools for political flyers. We call it junk mail.

47

Is Weather or Climate Changing?

Weather, the coming rains and cooler seasons that follow the 11, 15 and 18-year cycle peaks or hot spells, mainly control the current climate variations. This is an explanation of why the ecological "global warming" has passed its peak and now we have global cooling as the next cry for environmentalists.

The great 18.5-year cycle peak occurred in 1998, almost totally coincident with the 11.1-year hot sunspot cycle, the four-year business cycle and the great 26,000-year climate cycle.

Winter of 2000-1 on average around the country was 20% colder than many in the past 50 years and persisted, according to the weather bureau. Winter of 2001-2 was much cooler east of the Rockies to the coast. Even Europe and lands into Istanbul were placed under heavy snows by the weather god.

That was one of the reasons the shortage of energy and natural gas created such political furor. It was a manipulated shortage in 2000.

It is reported that in the 6th and 17th century Europe, it was bitterly cold, but that in the 9th through 13th centuries it was warm enough to support English citrus, Norwegian wine and the tulip industry in the lowlands. Suppose they thought about Global Warming during the 400 years of warm climate since the little ice age?

48

Who's Responsible for Depressions?

Politically, neither major political, nor minor party has mastered the business cycle of recessions and then boom times. Alan Greenspan, not discrediting him at all, merely tracks the extreme economic activities and demand for capital/cash into various sectors. He has a balancing act to do. Identifying the stage of any cycle and reading about the consequences of these major cycles for your business is part of manning the tiller of your business. This is the short-term seasonal variation business uses.

Andrews has been forecasting these events for 30 years under various governors and chairpersons. Until recently, Greenspan had been interpreting the numbers well. Now they want to "throw the bum out," Greenspan, just because he took away the punch bowl and didn't cut interest rates and add money to the banking system in 2000, he became *persona non grata*. "Off with his head, cried the queen," and the knights of Wall Street all nodded in agreement. What a bunch of spoiled investors and money managers. They know the market goes down too. But their egos are at stake as managers and advisors. These people dominate the psychological indicators of the Investors Intelligence newsletter. They perform similar to the public over-boisterousness during the final rallies, selling and dumping into the final lows to keep losers off their investment portfolio lists.

The nation's economy tracks the cycle with a lag time of about six months, before the volume of actual trade in dollar sales begins to break down. For retail stores, the up tick-in sales may take only three months after the major low occurs, while hard goods manufacturers may require nine to twelve months before seeing the up-tick in volume and profits reappear.

Neither Communistic theory nor free enterprise principles can control the cycles! Under the "right to fail" as well as prosper and to own property principle, still found in America, the economic and social winners far exceed those of the planned economy concept. The right to keep the winnings and spend the gains as one sees fit is far more of an incentive than the socialist idea that no one can be fired nor be forced to be creative or productive.

Congress alone shows it has little value in its legislative practice of legalizing trends. It can stifle enterprise with bad laws and high taxes, or specific industry taxes to inhibit certain sectors of business. These are unconstitutional, but then no one seems willing to challenge them at this time. Many of the laws created by legislatures are from proposals by an industry or a segment of an established industry to validate their control over its service or product to maintain their oligopoly positions.

The fewer the government agencies which interfere with production in this society, the more creative our society will be in meeting the needs, preferences and desires of the consumers. Capitalism and consumerism are much the same. Political philosophies of how to achieve a great society managed by elitists educated at the politically correct schools are an anachronism.

The philosophy that government owes one a house, food, job and health care is a socialist idea right out of the Communist Manifesto by Karl Marx and Freidrick Engels ("To each according to his ability...") No one is born equal in ability to another, only in the eyes of the law before the bar of justice as found in the U.S. of A. That law point is not fully implemented in the U.S. of A and never can be.

Winners get more privileges than the loser who is on the dole/food welfare, stamps, etc. The socialist demands for more pay for less work for the individual, who still does not want to be held responsible for the quality and quantity of his work, is a fallacy of socialism. If you have not seen or experienced socialism in operation, first hand, you may not want to believe how disreputable it has become to those who live with it daily. It is the lowest level of any organized society that has been devised since the cave man began a clan in this age of man. Everything is theoretical, not real, and not very workable.

This socialist and liberal philosophy will change and become noticeably less important in the next decades that follow as socialism is waning. This assumes the political leadership at the turn of the millennium gets taxes and social programs under control and wins the battle against a resurgent Islam fundamentalist population now salted in the western nations with Mosques.

We have been invaded and these Mosques will maintain control of these religious followers until the signal to rise up and take over in the name of Allah and Muhammad is given. Their goal is to take over the land, destroy the Capitalist western civilization and impose Muhammad's thoughts and the Koran, while denying any other than the Islam religion. The Koran would prevail and the clerics would rule. It's a holy war.

New ethic values must prevail and the nihilistic regression of Islam destroyed. It seems strange to have this philosophy so well indoctrinated into the Muslim minds when, with all their oil revenues, without western civilization being supplied, they would still be walking with their camels around the black gold goo of the deserts. This is self-immolation to the nth degree, a destruction of their own culture they are seeking to revive. Their talents seem 13 centuries behind the times. They could dispose of their culture of hate and destroy and turn their students into useful creative modern day individuals. They could become politicians, statesmen, engineers, contractors and scientists.

They could leave the past of the desert sands of history and move onto a new plane.

Still the entrepreneur can take notice of the retail change in monthly or even week-to-week statistics and the leading up-move of the stock markets. This gives the signal to get positioned for new orders and better business conditions. Consumerism leads the economy when it is at the turn. Watch for the shoppers at the store to signal that consumers are spending again.

Businessmen and government agencies release statistical charts interpreting the stage of the cycle by up to three months after the facts are in. They aren't perfect, but they do give national perspectives to local problems. Living in one region, and not noticing changes occurring in other regions, leaves a void. Cycle changes can be used to track the new direction, once a top or bottom is reached, which applies in most centers around the world.

Any forecasting based on such government charts is 90% guess, while 10% is intuitive "hunch" based on repeating patterns of similar data (especially if it is noted almost exactly 20 years ago). The problem is they are valid comparisons only if the inquirer asks the right questions, includes the important factors and are not too many months from the accumulated old data.

Once the bottom reversal pattern appears and is confirmed by other indices and bankers by improving loan terms, there is this lead time when planning and training which should get under way promptly.

One way to understand the evidence of a serious reversal is in the responses to advertising directed at customers. When consumers start to respond to specials and advertisements, then this confirms the upturn of the cycle.

This concept is as applicable to the stock markets as it is in daily business management of employees and products. It is the consumer attitude toward being willing to spend after hard times or in reverse after the peak of the good times. Their hesitancy or greedy response signals the stage of the cycle.

Sales, employment, interest rates, competition and profits follow the cycle. The businessman must be ready to act when the turn occurs. When your banker wants to charge a higher interest rate for your loan, you know things are getting a little too boisterous in the trade.

If you do not know what to expect at the various stages of the cycle, then you may be making the wrong decision, emotionally yielding to the pressures of the times to follow the crowd.

In future editions, Andrews will try to identify the new patterns and the stronger more elaborate changes in the new economy. Selective industries and the new technologies will become leaders in the new cycle once the big low is reached in the economy and markets.

As a business person, you may be enthusiastically reordering larger quantities of product and materials, hiring new people for new projects and borrowing at those slightly higher interest rates just as the market and economy are topping.

It is a characteristic of major tops to be extremely optimistic just before the disappointments begin.

The old rule still applies "When government discovers the problem and begins to react with investigations and legislation, the problem has been bypassed by the free flow of information by an informed public just like in the financial markets." Government acts only after the facts are in.

At the other position as stock markets decline and mortgage rates rise, retrenchment follows while others are building new plants and hiring with long-term visions of great prosperity. "They must be reading something that is not published, not a government report, not a purview of the FRB and they must know something the rest of us don't know," you may think.

"Business is not that good and job prospects are not easy to find," you may grumble into your coffee. It is time for the curious and competitive managers to investigate, to learn why things are not confirming the usual recovery business plan. It is a time to be cautious when results turn mixed.

In the current 2002 environment, the falling interest rates, instead of the usual rising rates, signals a different kind of a market is expected into the next 18 months before the mid-term 2002 elections. This requires extra concern simply because the consumer is back buying again, and now layoffs seem so far away. Too many optimists are still out there and too few who are willing to work hard and give value for their day's pay.

The big dilemma today is whether to follow the crowd or review the business plan to find a justification for greater expansion and/or higher risk. It is admirable to stick one's neck out and take a risk, but don't do it emotionally just because other entrepreneurs are showing disregard for the consequences.

How to act decisively to maximize the advantage of your product, site locations, demand, growth and how to lower the risk but maximize the gains confronts every executive. Go with the flow of the times or choose to fight the winds of change, means leaders must tack into the opportunity to again align the business with the market's needs.

There is one thing this time, in this winter of 2001-2 that signals that something is wrong! Chairman Alan Greenspan, of the FRB, lowered discount rates twice in January 2001. For a 1% decline in discount rates at a time when it was becoming evident the tight money policy and higher interest rates were used to curb the inflation of speculation in ".com" stocks and internet Initial Public Offerings, nothing happened. The market kept faltering and falling.

Spokespersons contend the Feds must lower interest rates again. Greenspan's fight has been against inflation, not in stimulating economic growth. He is still battling the windmills of imagined problems! He will not be reappointed to the FRB on expiration of his current tenure.

What of the results of lowered Federal Funds rates after a third rate cut? Still not enough to swing the market to the heavens again! So, what is wrong with the Monetarist Theory of interest rate manipulation and pump priming of Keynesian Theory?

According to Ned Davis Research, within 6 months following the third rate cut, an average of 13.4% rally maximum occurs, and in 12 months 24.9%. The maximum in 12 months since 1921 was 42.8% from the July 1982 market rally. The slowest was 1.5% from July 1980. April 30, 1991 was 16.3% off the 18-year lows. January 31, 1996 was up 24.9% and November 17, 1998 was up a 21.1% general gain (off the four-year cycle lows). October 20, 1933 was only 9.7% while in February 7, 1930 a loss of -35.4%. But remember, we are heading into an 18-year-cycle crash low. A 50% correction from the previous high may target the NASDAQ composite index for a bounce, not the DJIA.

49

Long-Term Market Trend Reversal Signals, a Look at the Future

Discount FRB Interest Rates

With the hope of lowered interest rates, a brief market rally followed in January 2000. It failed to stop the decline in stock prices, or increase hard goods production and orders. Industrial production had been on the decline since late August 2000, just following when the 18.5-year cycle made its economic lag top.

Capacity utilization made its peak in May and June 2000 right where expected on the top after the four-year cycle, two months after the NASDAQ stock market topped in the speculative blow-off in April, four months before the Crash.

The market cycles will be healthy and strong through 2002, when some recovery highs may well be noticed to be nearly as strong as earlier highs into 2003.

The old song that it takes six months to see the markets turn may hold true in the long run, but this decline (correction) was obviously going to take stock market prices much lower and in turn business profits and sales, since the major cycle peak in August 2000.

Failing to resume buying in the rallies was the "bail-out" signal in the stock market. Greenspan's reputation was to follow Paul Volcker, his predecessor, by "breaking the back of inflation," like the devaluation of the currency was found in the 70's on into 1982. The inflation began with the Great Society of President Johnson in 1966 when borrowing for the social programs began. Dollar devalued!

When mortgage rates hit 18% and gold nearly a thousand dollars an ounce ($850 was reported) in 1982, inflation ended. Gold was at 25% of the high in '82 and looking like it is ready again in 2002 for a rally of consequence or a 50% rally and is also a signal of an inflation of the dollar currency. As long as investors abroad prefer the American stock exchanges, the dollar will remain strong. Should the dollar falter, the Crash will be far more severe. Precious metals will prosper again only if dollars are replaced by Euros or Pounds. Neither appears to be threatening at publication. Resistance appeared at $300 oz.

How can that be when we are afloat in tax excesses and high unemployment levels? Take a look at the biological problems with our food supplies, illnesses, prescriptions and the declining populations. Without the undocumented immigration, our population would be stagnating.

Why do Chairman Greenspan's data and charts fail to predict the level of the markets and interest rates as well as other government economic research and banker's projections of business activity? Falling interest rates are usually bullish for the market. Why has this not worked this time?

Remember, FRB data and charts only track what the cycle of economic activity does. They cannot give the U.S. economy instructions to expand or contract. They like to think it is so, though.

This is the error of Communist and Socialist central planning beliefs. In a sense, all central planning has come from the belief that the elite know what's best. The author will concur with maybe 10% of that thinking, but not down to managing how much eggs will cost and who gets the last dozen on the shelf. Remember too, Keynes was educated during a period of socialistic prosperous entrepreneurs after WW I when socialistic ideas were in vogue.

What most forecasters fail to recognize is that similar events as do occur here are also happening in nearly every other western nation simultaneously and in most domestic cities. Track their market indices regarding their economic trends.

Most fundamentalist market advisors believe that the U.S. markets control the other markets in other countries. The sensitive nature of the U.S. market may lead to sluggish markets elsewhere, but not meaningfully.

Sometimes Japan, but at other times it is Hong Kong or London, which will lead the turn within a few hours before our markets are even open. Cycles are natural events. Fundamentals then follow on. Hence, the phrase "the market leads the economy." One must be alert to the true rules, not subterfuges.

That's the characteristic of a major cycle. The same goes for the four-year business cycle. Most business leaders like to make plans based upon trends affecting their business and to borrow to expand their business operations when the sales volume (minus costs shows a profit figure or at least a lessening of the losses) each year. When it is growing he wants to maximize his profits and suggests, in his mind, an approaching profitable year again.

When it comes to the eighteen (18.5)-year cycle (which peaked in 1998), the half wave is 9.3 years of growth, then 9.3 years of difficult marketing and net profits following the peak month. Often by observing charts or data reports, we may be misled by one good month in the business or the economy that is merely just a good month, not a trend change which usually takes three months of improved (or declining earnings at a top) to signal a reversal. Knowing where to expect the top or bottom we can be there ready to profit from the new trends.

Some investment policies are only applicable to stages of the various cycles. The Buy and Hold concept begins as the stock and the markets begin to make narrow trading ranges with PE ratios nearer to their historical low levels of 9-12 times earnings. These are the accumulation levels for the big rally as final liquidations are bought by savvy investors, from tired-of-it-all investors. These are usually found in the 18,

15, 11, and four-year lows following the last big base or low price narrow trading range of at least two weeks.

Some stocks respond more with one cycle or another, or when several merge together with the four-year cycle lows. Study the history of
the stock at the preceding period nearer to these lows in the past markets. Data bases and chart books are available if you look for them.

The base lines should be months long when a stock price refuses to
go lower in spite of the bad news. A change of management or product
line shift, perhaps a merger is announced and is the signal for increasing positions on the cheap. Coming out of fiscal bankruptcy with a
favorable court decision should be researched and confirmed so that
the risk is clearly low and the gains will become maximized.

Buy the rumor, sell on the good news. This is a good slogan should
you hear the rumor of a change in earnings, management, product line,
merger or some event that turns the company around. A risk is there,
but all life is a risk. Limit it to the loss you might take should the price
return to the previous lows of the past year or quarter. When the news
hits the market, the second day after it is in the papers or electronic
reports, the greatest short-term gain is ready to be taken.

Very often, the price will drop back over months to test the preceding lows hence management must prove itself under the new conditions. If it looks good after the sell down is confirmed, with a higher
low in place, consider whether you want to continue to buy this stock.
Buy the dips if you find you like the way it is acting by building its volume and price together in the same direction.

Therefore, Andrews sees the next major economic low in 2010, that
is, when the economy begins to reawaken. Before that low, we will
have the four-year lows in 2000, 2004 and 2008, national election
years. In between, we may find a 4.5-year low from the previous nine-
year peak (half-wave of the 18.5-year cycle) which market technicians
often call a double bottom buying point or the mid-point of the nine-
year down move. Often this period is called consolidation.

A weak recovery in the second half of 2002 may confuse many investors and businessmen. Yet, fortunes have been made before by aggressive investors, buying into the disaster lows. When the high volume drops in panic market selling period with an hourly ticker reading over 900 and preferably when 1200 is reached, the risk falls rapidly for a strong bounce to follow.

Then, the next move will be to higher prices in equities. Inflating commodities and with the price of gold and mining stocks making a better price run suggest a deflating dollar and economic depression conditions.

The following final and major rally for this 18-year cycle period is projected to run through 2002. The economic condition or pattern in the following decline or sell-down will be reported as a Panic.

Then, it will be a sell down with recurring tight money, higher unemployment, and smaller banking accounts among the working population and with political unrest showing in the campaigns. Two-step cycle drops and are characteristics of Bear markets and expected here too into the 2008-10 lows.

CRB Raw Materials Index

Falling prices in recent years have reached an apex low as shown on the CRB (Commodity Research Bureau Index). Unable to fall farther, as is likely with low energy prices, the breakout level is likely to be to higher prices and inflation, which is also deflation of the dollar.

Gold did a technical break out of its downtrend on May 11, 2001 suggesting higher prices. Observe the changes in prices by early January 2002 which if a double bottom or higher low occurs; it is a modest buying signal. The side-wise price consolidation around the low of $268 oz. into the new year confirms the breakout as a higher low. In February 2002, gold reached $300 oz. but could not hold above $300. Until it does, great inflation will be controlled.

Bloomberg charts the CRB Raw Industrial Materials Index as an indicator (commodities).

Industrial Production rate growth usually peaks out at the 6% to 7.5% level and bottoms out at near 0% at most four-year lows while the 18-year lows are greater than -4% in the face of plant closings of marginal manufacturers.

Dow Jones Industrials chart (proprietary of Wall Street Journal)

At this writing, the 9200 of March 22, 2001 lows have held. They were tested on September 21, 2001. The economy has grown since then and it is unlikely this low will be checked again. If it does, then the economy will have had devastating consequences and serious recovery problems may be prolonged. A double top is likely to be the maximum, at least for this 2002-3 top.

The NASDAQ Composite Index

The NASDAQ Composite is a measure of speculation since it is composed mostly of new and untested smaller stocks. In the current economic speculation, the NASDAQ outmaneuvered the conservative dividend paying stocks, and confirmed the speculative nature of the times.

It is paying the price with drops of over 90% from some stocks' peak in values. Higher prices are expected for the stronger leaders, which achieved good revenue flows, continue to hold value. None are free of risk because they are just now being tested. The strong ones will survive to lead again into the remainder of the decade.

Mutual Funds Cash Positions

The mutual funds cash position peaked in July 1982 at 12% and eight years later near the end of the Reagan Administration, it peaked at 13%, the signal of a major 18-year market low. As of late September '01, it was below 4%, and buying followed.

Historically, it made its high in October 1990, as the economy reached for its 18.5-year cycle low at 12.9% which was the market buy point. These advisory services are close to the public attitude so far as the psychological confidence occurs. They too buy into tops because so much cash is coming in and they finally sell into lows as investors try to raise cash. Sometimes the manager can use cash or bond funds to park cash until a good buy point is reached.

Get that urge to buy? Then it is likely a market top, unless you know your own instincts better than the other investors. A washout bottom in a high volume decline on opening, followed by a recovery nearly to the old closing price or index, perhaps with a small positive close is usually a strong Buy Signal.

When the market completed its final run in March 2000, it was at its low of 4% Mutual Funds cash position. In March 2001 it was still at a low at 5.4% suggesting more severe selling was still ahead.

Any rallies would be met with selling opportunities for knowledgeable investors. In light of the many options still held among the high tech, internet, .com companies, any rally approaching their old strike price that is, where they could counter their tax burden from other sales or show a profit, is likely to be their profit taking point.

Such extremes vary only slightly by perhaps 1% more or less at major turns. They are trustworthy.

Jobless Rate, monthly

Increasing joblessness continues until the economic low has passed by about two quarters. It is valid only as a confirming index. In today's economic practices, with the unemployment insurance programs, early retirement, and contract labor programs along with temporary worker programs, the actual cycle top is delayed on any statistical chart until the employee seeks a new job. This seems to run about a year lagging behind actual number counts. It also lags about a year at major lows.

Politically, this often hides any current political administration from taking the blame.

Producer Price Index and the core rate of inflation

When this index breaks below 50%, it signals order declines where lay-offs and the shutdown of production lines begins. After peaking in the 80% level several years ago, it seems destined to punch in close to 30% level before a business pick-up begins with new orders (in 2008). This affects the employment levels in many areas where industrial plants dominate the labor market. Watch this index since it leads 3-6 months before the pipeline of supplies hits local markets.

Psychological Indicators

Investors Intelligence offers one of the better guides for tracking trends. It gives one of the more accurate longer-term indicators of economic and market health to the extent of speculative activity. Speculative activity is usually found in the final year of an 18-year cycle into its peak, about the tenth year from its preceding major low.

Bearish Investment Advisors usually max out when the market is at high levels with only 22 to 24% of the advisors being bearish or negative about buying stocks. When the advisory services have a negative attitude on the market direction, reaching around 50% bearish, then is when we can expect a reversal off a low stock and index level and it gives a good long-term buying opportunity.

The current readings for the Bearish Advisors in May 2001 was 37.2%, after reaching a maximum in mid April of 42%. This suggests an intermediate term low, not a major low has occurred. In early July '01 the bearish advisor reading of 25.5% was almost to the sell low point. Again in January 2002 it reached 22-23%, ready for a sell down.

Why not bullish advisors? Because most advisory services are bullish therefore they are less reliable. These readings may appear to be conflicting. It's at bottoms where we will find terror and despair, not tops.

Rains begin to falter in 2006

During the recessive period of 2006-2008, rains begin to reappear in many of the western states and the La Niña prevails. Usually, rains mean greater agricultural productivity and lower food prices. One of the great components of good times is good seasonal rainy weather. When it dominates the world production regions, prosperity reigns. But when drought appears, recessions worsen usually creating shortages and higher prices. Into 2007 rains will be more abundant in the U.S. The rains will be the worst on the west coast and mountain states in 2006-09. Then into year 2011, the droughts and summer heat reappear.

Short Interest Ratio

Another leading indicator is the Short Interest Ratio on the NYSE. When it reaches a low of 3.4 to 3.6% there is usually a sharp, short covering rally.

Squeezing the short positions often is the first signal of bottoming and takes some three months for a test of the lows to recur. Once this higher low or double bottom has evolved, a greater rally is expected to turn into the test of old highs. This can be very profitable to alert investors.

If the first rally fails at 50% of the previous down move, then another sell-off will take the markets and the economy into lower levels of activity. Major bottoms usually have a three-wave bottom, and intermediate lows are noted for double bottoms, or for spike down lows over about a three-month period. Perhaps even more significant is the IBD (Investors Business Daily), a financial publication from Westwood, California, gave a sell signal.

The three-wave bottoms may be in non-DOW Index stocks such as Utilities (with FRB intervention in money supply or interest rates), Blue Chip and Mid-Cap stocks may turn early, the mass of stocks then bottom on the second wave down and the final right shoulder bottom likely includes the laggards which have fewer short positions to be covered. Utilities usually move up with falling prime interest rates.

Using the 200-day moving average versus the 50-day average, the latter should cross above the 200-day average before the buying signal is valid. Combined with various funds, the index reflects the sum value of the fund's issues. Currently, winter 2002, they are testing the downtrend line off the tops of the previous highs in a down-trending market. Should this price level hold then we should experience a significant rally into the peak due in late 2002-3. Ideally, the 50-day average and prices should cross above their 200-day average as the buy point and in reverse the sell point in the longer wave market peak.

Real Estate and Construction

One of the most accurate economic cycles is the 18.5-year cycle. At its peak, new permits and sales of existing homes, marriages and optimism prevail. Money is easy to get at low interest rates, hard to get at peak of the rates. The desire to own a new home seems to surge periodically, and often the owners overpay believing they will improve their income and a secure economic condition prevail during the coming years.

At bottoms in demand, usually at market lows, after divorces, forced sales of homes, unemployment and illnesses falling real estate prices may prevail along with droughts; sluggish manufacturing, retail merchandise sales, slow construction, and a reduced immigration.

Older neighborhoods age and often become rentals with lower valuations. One other characteristic is that in the economic weakness, and when near to the lows, famous and well-known personalities are reported as passing. Down-zoning may occur, degrading values of many properties.

Three wave tops and three wave bottoms are a characteristic

Major turning points follow in severe down-selling in high volume. The problem is the personal psychological attitude of being too bullish at tops and too bearish at bottoms, regardless of stock prices, usually interferes with the decision making process.

The mid-point or second sell-down often becomes the head of a reverse head and shoulders formation hence it would be the ideal buy point. The third wave down is usually a right inverted shoulder, as technicians talk, and is the final buying point.

Rotation of leadership may be noted for the laggards on the third wave down. Stronger than market stocks and new leaders will turn with the first low or the second one as the head-down spike low turns up in heavy churning volume.

Out of the past, look to the future!

50

The Coming Energy Crisis is Here, Now!

It started in California in the year 2000. It was a hot spring, dry and burgeoning with illegal immigrants crossing the borders looking for seasonal work and migrating in greater numbers than ever before. It was destined to be one of the hottest summers in many generations. Many immigrants died in the desert. It was also destined to be the end of the era of Global Warming ideas.

It was a time when electricity had been deregulated after 1996 in California. It was at the peak of the housing construction 18-year cycle and it was the season of the 11.1-year sunspot cycle, which always produces high winds and Santa Ana firestorm conditions in the west.

The four-year cycle had made its top in the early spring of the year 1998. The next peak is in 2002. Wow! How can anyone be so precise and confident? No problem! This is the way life is, a routine generation-to-generation, cycle-to-cycle. We cannot forever be crossing the great void without end or mindless direction. Man would finally die in the struggle never having found anything familiar or helpful.

The order of the solar system has remained constant, only man cannot remember, having such a short life span and being part of the problem of solar life forms.

Power bills suddenly ballooned to triple and some to sextuple, above ordinary summer levels. Forest fires abounded and the hot winds blew offshore as Santa Ana winds and later they blew eastward over the mountain passes to the eastern prairies as Chinooks. The hot high pressure winds moved into Chicago and New York regions. Central cities accumulated heat daily and the terrible compression winds brought temperatures into the 120° F level in late afternoons.

The winds have always blown this way and always will, no matter how the ecologists proclaim their dominance and desires. Around the world there were fires as seen by astronauts and on satellites viewing the regions. Environmentalists were aggressively pushing their agendas in the media and in articles.

Everything was burning along with our national forests in the west. Without air-conditioning and cooling systems, it was unbearable inside factories, shops and homes. Big city residential buildings were furnaces of accumulated daytime heat for several days with elder citizens cooped up in non-air conditioned units.

A rate price cap for electricity was held in place, but wholesale prices were free to float, as Loretta Lynch, Chairman of the California Public Utilities Commission decided, forcing utilities to buy in the spot market only. That was the law she and the legislature had devised and it was signed by then Governor Pete Wilson. Does not make much sense does it? But politicians make strange bedfellows at times. We need a total and scientific revision to economic and market theory as well as rules based on sound principles, not political hay.

The winter of 2000-1 was about 20% colder than normal, according to NOAA weather forecasters. It took a bit more energy to keep the water pipes from freezing. The summer of 2001 was barely warmer than 2000, suggesting a blow-off had occurred in the Global Warming. The winter season looked more like the 26,000-year cycle of climate maximum (Global Warming) had passed. Glaciers were forming chilly weather last found nearly 10,000 years ago. It is believed solar heating had maximized in year 2000.

It was an illustrious year 2000, after all. Most survived the peak of the hottest climate since the glaciers started to melt noticeably in 1870 to open the mountain valley lands to small populations some five millenniums past. The little Ice Age in the early part of the second millennium was the last gasp of the cold part of the 26,000-year cycle. Few, if any of us, remember the year 24,000 BC when it was very hot in another age of man. Archaeologists are finding evidence of such civilizations today.

Archeologists are probing the Antarctic for evidence of another ancient culture called Atlantis, fabled to have been as great as this world's culture. Where is Atlantis? Big secret!

Since the NOAA people still have no premise of what causes hot weather, cold weather, rainstorm lows and hurricanes, winds and the El Niño stratified weather around the world, how can we expect the EPA (Environment Protection Agency) and ecologists to get the answers right?

Much of the environmentalist agenda is not for the betterment of the environment but to gain control over the political system indirectly through bureaucratic methods. It is a socialistic/ communistic ploy, that's all. The dupes who believe this idea that they are protecting the earth against the inroads of man are surely as misguided as a roman candle lighted by a nervous six-year old. The consequences they do not understand nor care about, except it is fun to see the light scream into the heavens. If the candle balls get aimed towards the observers, it could create havoc.

Environmentalism was aimed at the people, the citizens, by a wayward band of self-centered boomers, led by the Sierra Club and others. It is aided and abetted by the radical Green Party from Germany, Earth Liberation Front emanating from the forests of Oregon around the universities. They make arson attacks against businesses, which, they believe, threaten the environment. "It is one of the most dangerous terrorist groups," according to the FBI. Note the use of the word, "terrorist." We have them in the U.S. too, not just from the Middle-Eastern sand-locked nations.

Its sister organization—"The Animal Liberation Front" has been vandalizing across the country since 1997 destroying research labs as another Nihilistic movement. One day they may have another organization crying out like the HIV victims did, for help against this antisocial behavior for a medicine or pill to cure a new disease called "victimizing." They will not allow others the opportunity to anticipate medical needs by using animals for testing of new drugs, nor for their testing on humans. How do these people get so mentally shortchanged?

Perhaps, this last big swing of achievement of mankind into the new millennium was so fast that the broad populations around the world could not digest and comprehend the values for new discoveries. The school systems seem more bent on teaching hate against progress that they have not been teaching basics of the 3 R's for several generations and it has finally caught up with cultures. Islam is still living and thinking in terms of the first days after Muhammad imposed his ideas on local tribesmen and enforced acceptance by the sword. Attempts are being made to make the Islamic religion dominant in America and Western nations by indoctrinating in the schools. It is rumored that text books are already printed and are expected to be distributed and used in seminars for over seventh grade students to teach Islam and the Koran. In California, this brings the religious wars right into the top half of the local newspapers. Unfortunately, if the Christian news is printed it is likely to be put on the back inside pages near the bottom.

To study the history of weather beyond 1900 is an area of forbidden research because the recalcitrant people are out of the loop and without proper education. Even Carole Browner, EPA Administrator under the Clinton Administration, lifelong member of Sierra Club, never had a clue, but she had friends in high places and could talk a blue streak. Even with the facts they do not want to accept responsibility for their environmental decisions and actions against society.

It is even doubtful that her replacement Administrator Christine Todd Whitman, former governor of New Jersey, sees the facts in any different light. It's the same old bureaucracy in and out of Washington doing the same old thing only with a different spin. The public is tired of this! Until there is a change of heart-felt beliefs among the concerned, there is likely very little that will change. Most likely, it will be a generational change as the passing of hardliners wanes. What will replace environmentalism?

That is the most discouraging thing about our state of national affairs. No matter who gets elected, it seems, the bureaucrats, educated at the same old universities all congregate around the water fountains in government agencies thinking the same tired old ideas that were never proven under communists Marx and Engels, but were handily used to gain power over the public taxpayers. Election 2000 produced new names but kept the old projects, many just changing the name plates on their office doors.

In fact, Carole Browner and her lieutenants in the EPA strangled many industries and the nation with their take-over of agencies, their history of good work then twisted the goals with decisions based on personal agendas and few serious "scientific" studies.

The Scientific Method is not limited to Ph.D.'s in the hard sciences. It is a logical method using facts that can be duplicated by others using various proven formulas and obtaining an acceptable common repeatable conclusion by others.

This is why Browner destroyed their hard disk files (government property) by reformatting them just before the new President Bush took over in January 2001. There was a court order prohibiting them from destroying the records pending a civil court suit against the agency. As arrogant as the rest of the agencies, staffed by the liberal agenda thinkers, Browner gave the order to clear the justification she and her agencies had taken to restrain our society from ever again leading the world in workmanship creativity.

One of the other problems has been the shredding and loss of documentation in the past eight years by the Clinton Administration. Without documents, who can be penalized or punished by the law of the land? The Clintons got away with it! Will this precedent prevail for the next 1000 years? The liberal social thinkers are destroying their correspondence and "scientific" justification for their inept decisions, some call "junk science." Academics have accepted this politically correct thinking to maintain budgets, positions, security, rank and power.

What is more worrisome is the failure of our elected Senators, Congressmen and Justice Department officials from both major parties from acting against these illegal acts, and to consider real campaign finance reform, to vote to impeach, or even investigate and hold hearings with real intent to prosecute them for their incursions.

Just for the record, to discover how they manipulated events to reach their own goals would have been a great history lesson. We do not teach much history in the public schools anymore and apparently not in this society or the news media. The spin is the thing, derived neither from facts nor deep analysis. The shallow understanding and reporting of events has created a mob mentality by the powerful media elements and government agencies.

51

Water Rights of the West

Without water, dams, reservoirs, generators, power grids and irrigation systems, the west would be rangeland for cows, sheep, goats, antelope, elk, deer, wolf, bear and rabbits. It would be open country for the owl, raven and crow from the Missouri to the Central Valley of California. It would eliminate most of the northwest.

The battle is brewing by the ecological interests of the Federal government and the anti-civilization special interest groups who are denying farmers and ranchers the use of surface water and snow melt stored from rains to irrigate their ranches. It is our Achilles Heel. There would be no water for Los Angeles, San Francisco, Portland, Seattle and no Las Vegas. There would be little energy generated for the cities and industry of the west. Water is a product of climate and weather, not SUV's. Without it the lands become deserts like we still find Bedouins leading camels in picturesque National Geographic Society magazines.

We would have fish, but no one would be permitted to get into the lands to fish. We would have no endangered species because none could verify there was trouble in the drought or rain-driven lands.

Forest fires would rage uncontrolled every hot season. None could extract the dead burned trees for lumber products or to build homes, manufacture furniture or heat, even a campfire.

The Indians could not live there because Fish and Wildlife Rangers would block their return. Bigfoot might multiply and hold the territory because he is so elusive.

Floods downstream would devastate the bottomlands, riverbanks and take out the bridges into New Orleans and the Mississippi delta. From the Canadian border, the Red River valley and the Great Lakes headwaters in Minnesota and Wisconsin, floods would destroy agricultural lands every year now productively feeding the nation. Fully half the nation's lands would be devoid of man and his talents to survive and develop fruitfully.

For what purpose should these small well-organized groups of anti-social and no growth throwbacks to Nihilism return the land to primitive wastelands? Why should small groups and judicial decisions of minority elements take precedence over the greater good of the nation's people? Why should their claims take preference over historical practices to turn society into their playground with edicts from Congressional laws and various confusing and conflicting, political agenda?

Why should publicly built dams and resources be denied for use by the public just because some small group objects and wants to keep it for their personal playground without paying in their own dollars for the right to hold title? Why should the government dispossess legitimate title-holders because of the whims of some Federal cabinet members and politicians?

There is a strange mindset here. It is foreign to our freedoms and national interest. From what source could such an anti-social attitude develop? These are the people indoctrinated in the post WW II era, against the general good of the population. Theirs is a philosophy very similar to that being taught today in the Arab and Muslim schools run by the cleric. Hate America! Hate progress, new ideas and science. Why should such an attitude, taught by religious zealots, flow around the world in the name of Islam? Is this some exogenous force imposing hate on society or man going mad from an increasingly complex society? A reminder to freedom lovers—one of the great concepts of America that is fundamental to its success is the right to own land inviolate.

Where this has prevailed, prosperity has followed and creativity overcomes restraints of religion and culture of the people's past.

52

Let's Look at a Bit of Historical Fact

The Chinese population began to expand and organize into Cantons around 4000 BC while Europeans moved into the Norwegian Peninsula and British Isles. Asian lands began to appear farther north as the ice melted and populations moved away from the warm oceans. Just a bit of forgotten history?

That was the beginning of global warming and had nothing to do with automobile exhaust, CO^2, farm and wild animals exuding methane, burning of fossil fuels, or the beauty of the land being despoiled by an electrical generator plant, a factory or houses on the edge of a big city high rise.

The California Public Utility Commission approved the spot-bidding pricing system, but utilities were unable and not allowed to pass the added costs on to rate payer consumers. (We thought syndicalism and communism was dead. But here it is in action.)

There had not been a new refinery or electrical generating plant built in California for ever a decade. Many smaller units had been decommissioned and some were only allowed to operate when under extreme clean air conditions, usually in low demand periods. Still the environmentalists complained that they were polluting our clean air in Los Angeles and the central valley. Some in the Bay area were miffed by this occasional marginal generating station use.

Many energy projects were proposed but never approved because of the environmental impact requirements and the NIMBY (not in my backyard) restriction by many cities and counties. It was getting costly to remodel, update or build any new plants based upon big labor premiums of 35% and environmental make-work requirements and limitations.

Winter of 2000 was with roaming black-outs and had shaken the computer and energy dependant industries until they were shopping for new sites outside of the state. They wanted to get away from the socialist state regulations of the liberal democratic legislature and then Governor Gray Davis.

Meanwhile, the rapid growth of doubling populations had also nearly doubled the energy demand during the recent two decades. California has the record for being the most energy efficient state in the union.

Agriculture programs were devastated: Chicken hatcheries couldn't keep the eggs warm, food producers couldn't wash, dry and process their products, milk producers couldn't milk the cows, separate the cream, or manufacture ice cream, milk, butter, and cheese products. Production lines were stilled and wasted production had to be dumped. Hardly a business was unaffected financially and many had to close early on brownout days.

Many out-of-state of California residents, were subject to the same restrictions limiting new power plant construction, oil and gas exploration, refineries, and water use as in many areas of the nation.

The population rise and increasing energy use caught up to us in this 21st Century. California remains the lowest cost per capita consumer in the lower 48. We are discovering there is little excess energy capacity, not enough gasoline, prices are too high, and of course, it is colder in winter and hotter in summer than usual in Chicago, Dallas, Atlanta, New York City, D.C., San Francisco, San Diego, Los Angeles, Seattle, St. Louis and even the New England cities.

Still, higher prices have led to increased production and now lower prices given market efficiencies down the road a few years after the peak use. We were also expected to be in the throws of an economic crisis from the political and economic distortions of the election in 2000, as we begin to shrink the economy with this next 18-year cycle. WTC bombings hid the real problems until the elections of 2002 changed the subject and blamed the problems on the Republican Administration. The crisis was still developing in 2001-2.

Our phobias about the environment found the culprit to be the (SUV) sport utility vehicle, on a light truck chassis with limited smog requirements, which is "consumin' too much gas," as one senator said, averaging around 16 mpg., some as low as 12mpg.

Recently, buyers of SUV's have decided they have had enough vehicles so that factories are now shutting down and redeploying labor as demand falls. Ford is closing major plants and reducing their forces by 35,000 worldwide. It will take most of the next seven years to alter the problems of these displaced laborers who prefer to work to the dole. Yet, this is the goal of every political party and nation for that matter, to employ the labor in the most constructive manner possible to maintain prosperity. How can these leaders get the job done when they do not understand the secret of the cycles that govern our lives and our economies? This book had to be written, if we are to solve our problems with under-employment and too many good time years of not enough labor? Now that labor is in surplus, will the illegals without documentation, forged documents and planted aliens return to their home lands? Most must be forced to relocate at the end of the sword, the gun, the militia.

The SUV was born from the energy crisis of 1970's since light trucks could buy rationed gas anytime and the smog controls did not apply to the vehicles built on the truck chassis. Look for big changes now! New models expected in 2006-2008.

As industries reduce production, employees are furloughed or put on permanent leave, the plant is sold and production is moved to cheap labor lands (NAFTA) or WTO low cost centers. They are all tied together now since few will have any special advantage as our labor rates fall to equalize them to overseas valuations. With automatic machinery, our U.S. labor tends to be higher paid. Labor rates are higher than those using antiquated machinery and skills. Some skills are cheap as retired ship and construction scavengers overseas dismantle them or when using foreign flag vessels.

As usual, our first impressions are subjective and usually wrong being based not on facts but on the affect it has on our personal life or business. So it is with environmental beliefs and as to what is cause and what is effect.

Unintended consequences follow legislation that was intended to aid specific groups with their agenda benefiting unstated groups, noted in fine print. We are caught in the spider's web. The spider is shaking the grid to see if she is really fortunate enough to have found another victim for lunch.

53

Socialism Versus Capitalism

Will it never cease? With May Day around the world this past May 1, we found communists swarming in Australia, London, Paris, Berlin and around the globe complaining about the capitalist system "making a profit." The word "profit" seems to cause these people to go berserk like the Pavlovian dog salivating on the bell cue. Theirs is a half-truth that Capital has no value and only their labor does. If it were so, why do they seek budget and funding for their anti-capitalist projects like welfare, subsidized housing, homeless shelter, grants in aid, from the tax paying corporations and successful people? Jealousy, or just confused?

This is the problem with the socialistic concept of central planning intended for the "greater good" of all citizens. Under central planning, some citizens goof off, others are perpetually ill, many are incompetent, lots of paternalism, bad decisions go unpunished, nor is anyone likely to be fired.

Worst of all the engineers, scientists, doctors and the highly skilled get the same pay as the guy that occasionally sweeps the floor for his contribution, all at the same wage rate. This is the result of the Russian Communist and Marxist planners, Yugoslavian socialism, French socialist planning, and eastern European planning programs made by the appointed Marxist bureaucracy given the planning responsibility. Indonesian and Chinese communists follow the same textbook.

Apartments all look alike as do their vehicles, clothes, shoes and even bicycles, paint colors, etc. Variety is still the spice of life. Russian communism is still engrained in the public's mind—toilets on first floors with water supplies, living quarters in the rest of the six floors.

With no incentives, experts/specialists make no changes or variety decisions unless forced/authorized by the hierarchy/commissar. Why work on a new version of something that could overcome deficiencies or change with the times, when few would support the change and you might even get thrown out of the party for not being politically correct? There is no competition under central planning.

Only the deviants from the big plan of the central government get liquidated, and not from inefficiency, but from not being the politically correct, loyal Marxist folk who adhere to the philosophy of the day.

Fascism has come to America in the new name of liberal Democrat, the Arabian immigrants of Muslim faith, a few liberal Republicans and Independents, environmentalists and those with price control concepts. The fascism taught in the universities is about multiculturalism. They have their own anti-white folk departments which teach them that all their problems are caused by other folk, that they are the ones who led civilization out of Africa, or that they need quotas to compete, or are entitled to preferences, just because. Responsibility is not in their vocabulary. Now, with Islam and the Koran, they are the superior race and will govern with a vengeance, eliminate capitalism as their enemy, if their past proves their fierce religious style is anything but a return to 750 AD, the times when Muhammad was a sand rancher and goat herder. Things have not changed much for their thinking and economic prosperity have not adapted to scientific discoveries.

Fascism blossomed well in Russia against minorities, and in Germany against the non-Aryan folk. Even in recent years, the labor from foreign countries was only permitted to work in industrial factories with specific permission for a limited time. This is still being practiced in China, Pakistan and India. A reminder to all the pacifists:

Wars are fought by those who believe they have developed greater military skills than their neighbors and who want cheap slave labor, booty and other freebies left over after killing or enslaving the enemy. History should be a required subject in all schools in all nations—not just their local history, but world events, not revisionism to enhance their local beliefs, but others who have different beliefs.

54

How Does Totalitarianism Start?

We like to think that it wasn't our fault and that someone "snookered" our freedoms when we were working and enjoying life. Believe the Boy Scouts, there is never a time you can let your guard down and trust someone in power to protect your personal and freedom interests. "Be Prepared" at all times. Keep the guard up and well trained.

Back in the 1930's in the Great Depression when money was hard to get and inflation was taking what income that was available, surviving was the greatest instinct at our disposal. Most of us were looking for a better way to live, to have a free government and with good leadership, a set of ideals we could follow since ours were in need of updating.

We did not know that economic events, weather and our good health were not completely within our control. We trusted others to make the right decisions. That's why we elected these leaders to powerful positions of authority over us.

It was then that Adolf Hitler, the house painter, began to make speeches about how things ought to be and proceeded to gather around him people who were willing to follow his leadership. He held beer parties for the less fortunate, made speeches about doing something to better their lives and even gave them food, clothes, uniforms and holiday camps where they could send their children for an "education."

People supported him and his leadership, doing as they were told, contributing to his party.

He taxed industry heavily (shook down as some are doing today), raised money for a private army and burned the Reichstag, the capitol of the government where laws were passed. Without a place to meet elected representatives could not govern. He had made a deal with Von Pappen, the next most powerful member of Reichstag to be Chancellor with full powers. Aging General Paul von Hindenburg (WW I Field Marshall, Chief of Staff and second President of the German Republic) was getting tired of trying to form a government of splinter groups (called multi-culturalists).

He finally yielded to letting Hitler be the Chancellor. This is when Hitler took over the government because he had the troops and the public support. He burned the Reichstag (parliamentary building like our Congress). The existing government-elected officials were rounded up, put in prisons, denied any rights and many were killed.

Now that he was fully in charge and had trained youth at his beck and call (note the Muslim schools teaching hate America), he looted the libraries and burned their books, introduced racism against the Jewish people, confiscated their property and sent them off to camps, eventually to the Holocaust. His troops harassed their ethnic neighbors until they too and most of Europe were forced into the Third Reich under his control. His rallying cry was *he was creating a nation to last 1000 years.*

Hitler began to campaign against gun ownership, "dumbed" down the population with propaganda from Dr. Joseph Goebbels and indoctrinated the schools, taught that the Aryan people were destined to rule the world (substitute Islam today). Without weapons the Jewish people could not defend themselves, nor could any of the businessmen and bankers resist his take-over moves. He controlled the media, the newspapers and magazines so that only his ideas were promulgated. Everything was censored and had a Nazi spin. (Note the sameness of our AP,

UPI and the TV networks, to say little of our newspapers, movies and magazines.)

He had moved into South America and many nations of the world taking control using blocked currencies in exchange for raw materials and sold them war tools and manufactured goods. This was isolating the U.S., England, France, Canada and other developed nations limiting their market places.

His economic plan seems little different than the Chinese series of world bases and limiting the other nations from selling to China. We'll have to wait and see how this one develops to see if the Chinese are besting Hitler, and perhaps the Arabs best the Chinese.

Meanwhile, in the U.S. of A. we have developed Politically Correct ideas, non-thinking responses, Pavlovion (salivating dog) responses and buzz words of the socialist and Marxists (we have over 58 of them as avowed Marxists), elected to our highest offices in the Senate and the House of Representatives).

In other elected offices the Marxists are not counted. They, with their agents in the press, destroy the character of any person who opposes them, using false charges and innuendoes so that the public will no longer be opposed to their collectivist objectives.

We are bombarded daily with propaganda like that which Ph.D. propagandist Joseph Paul Goebbles created during the Hitler years. That objective today is still the taking over of this free government like Hitler and Stalin attempted in controlling Germany and Russia by the use of string of commissars and front agencies to manage and manipulate the voting public.

55

The High Risk Period is Year 2008-10

Rosie O'Donnell, the TV talk show hostess, advocates gun control on her show daily trying to make guns illegal. In an Internet Poll she took in the spring of 2001, used to promote her new magazine, Rosie asked her readers for their comments. They were mainly in the age group of 25-50, the group now controlling much of our economic, educational and political institutions. The results were surprising.

These are the numbers:

1. I'm for gun control.____3%

2. I think everyone has a right to own a gun with no restriction.____79%

3. I think it's okay to own a gun, provided the owner is licensed to carry.____3%

4. I think it's okay to own a gun, provided there are background checks at time of sale.____14%

Rosie recently took the test and registered a gun "to protect her children."

The people appear to be smarter than their entertainers and news publishers.

After the WTC bombing there was little gun control editorializing in the press. How soon will it resume?

Andrews projects a major degenerated failure of the European Economic Union even before it becomes fully operational. It is bureaucracy at its worst with the socialist and communist concepts intact from the glory days under Josef Stalin. Disarming the public is essential for populace control.

It will take time to reeducate the masses who like the freebies or wait for their demise. It seems that the peculiar thinking of these super-peasants, as a class, must derive the idea from the magnetic induction flowing around earth, for it is certainly not from logic or cause-to-effect thinking. Of course, they only want their fair share, right? "I'll take mine right out of the middle, the fillet, first!" Wouldn't you?

The line is drawn here. Cross it at your own risk. There is no room left for ideologies foreign to our Constitution. A purge is likely before new immigrants will be permitted.

DO NOT CROSS

About the Author

Robert Earl Andrews is an economist, consultant and amateur astronomer. He is a graduate from Cambridge College in Accountancy, Denison University in Economics, and did his graduate study at University of Michigan, Ohio State University in Economics, UCLA and College of Canyons in Astronomy. He taught business administration, accounting and economics at Cambridge, Muskingum and University of Nebraska.

He worked as a Management Engineer and consultant for Hughes, Northrop, North American-Downey, Rocketdyne and Cannon Electric; studied astronomy for fifty years as an amateur, defining forces that affect, economics, market pricing, weather and climate.

This book includes explanations of when in time, longer-term stock market and socio-economic maximums as well as major minimums can be expected to occur. Opinions of what is going to happen are based on historical events at the various stages of the cycles mentioned, and specific problems dominating the next decade of this country, of the world and into the next century.

Politically, this is a time of great social, economic and physical changes—a watershed period in time. Andrews has forecast well with as much as 98% accuracy in some research years in the past half-century of his work. For many of the more recent events his work was nearly 100% accurate. His research reports have been privately published to his clientele.

Any comments by the author referring to a person, company, trademark, brand, idea, or product was not intended to criticize, plagiarize, degrade or defame in any way. Comments were made as illustrations of events and about persons within the time frame of historical moments at various stages of economic, political, sociological and weather cycles.

Events were interpreted based on conditions of the times in which they occurred.

0-595-21984-5

www.ingramcontent.com/pod-product-compliance
Lightning Source LLC
Chambersburg PA
CBHW061353280526
45784CB00001B/238